How to be a Brilliant Trainee Teacher

This cheerful and accessible book is packed with direct and straightforward advice drawn from the author's extensive and successful personal experience as teacher-trainer, teacher and examiner. It sets out clear and practical guidelines to support your training and enhance your teaching, moving you directly towards a real understanding of how and why pupils learn and of how you can enhance your own progress.

It also offers reassurance and support with the difficulties which you might encounter through your training as a teacher. Why won't Year 8 actually do anything? Why do we have to read all this theory? I know my pace and timing need improvement, but what do I actually do about it? Why haven't I moved forward at all in the last four weeks?

It does this by:

- outlining strategies for organisation;
- exploring issues of personal development;
- demystifying areas often seen as difficult or complex;
- providing achievable and practical solutions;
- directly addressing anxieties.

Although a practical book, at its heart lie essential principles about good teaching and learning. It is anecdotal and readable, and may be dipped into for innovative lesson ideas or read from cover-to-cover as a short, enjoyable course which discovers exciting teaching principles in successful, practical experience.

The book is ideal for secondary trainee teachers, but the underlying principles about what makes a brilliant trainee teacher are applicable to primary trainees too.

Trevor Wright, University of Worcester, has been a successful teacher for about thirty years, and a trainer of teachers for about ten years. Ofsted inspectors describe his school teaching as 'uncommon, exemplary, extraordinarily effective'. His postgraduate teacher-trainees consistently evaluate their training as 'sup...   ...es as both teacher and teacher-traine'   en principle and practice on a day-t

Also by Trevor Wright:

How to be a Brilliant English Teacher

How to be a Brilliant Trainee Teacher

Trevor Wright

Illustrated by Shaun Hughes

Routledge
Taylor & Francis Group

LONDON AND NEW YORK

First published 2008
by Routledge
2 Park Square, Milton Park, Abingdon, Oxon OX14 4RN

Simultaneously published in the USA and Canada
by Routledge
270 Madison Ave, New York, NY 10016

Routledge is an imprint of the Taylor & Francis Group, an informa business

© 2008 Trevor Wright

Typeset in Sabon by
HWA Text and Data Management, Tunbridge Wells
Printed and bound in Great Britain by
TJ International Ltd, Padstow, Cornwall

British Library Cataloguing in Publication Data
A catalogue record for this book is available from the British Library

Library of Congress Cataloging-in-Publication Data
A catalog record for this book has been requested

ISBN10: 0–415–41109–2 (hbk)
ISBN10: 0–415–41110–6 (pbk)
ISBN10: 0–203–94507–7 (ebk)

ISBN13: 978–0–415–41109–7 (hbk)
ISBN13: 978–0–415–41110–3 (pbk)
ISBN13: 978–0–203–94507–0 (ebk)

UNIVERSITY OF CHICHESTER

Contents

	Acknowledgements	vi
1	Questions at an interview	1
2	Key journeys	19
3	Being a teacher	28
4	Being a trainee	42
5	Planning	85
6	Managing learning, managing classrooms	97
7	Reflection and evaluation	115
8	Being brilliant	127
9	Finishing and starting	150
	Suggested reading	167
	Index	168

Acknowledgements

I would like to thank my colleagues in the Institute of Education at the University of Worcester for their many expert suggestions and contributions to the preparation of this book.

With thanks also to Shaun Hughes for the illustrations and to Wendy Logan for the index.

Chapter 1

Questions at an interview

We all know about teaching. Individually, we are subjected to it compulsorily for at least eleven years, experiencing it and evaluating it day after day. We sit in classrooms thinking, 'This is good', or 'Blimey, I could do better than this myself.' Collectively, we are used to turning to schools to solve society's problems and even sometimes to blaming them for its ills. We have opinions and information about teaching that far exceed our relationship with any other profession. Teaching is the most visible of all occupations. It is also the most misunderstood.

Of course, teaching is an exciting profession. It is rewarding, varied, creative and challenging. It is unpredictable, funny and intellectually stimulating. It's not a fantasy job (rock star, astronaut) but it's the best real-world job available, if you can do it. Nevertheless, our perception of it is blighted by the illusion that we already understand it.

If you are to train as a teacher, you have to be able to answer the fundamental question 'Why do you want to teach?' You will be asked this at interview; but, more significantly, you should be asking yourself anyway. A common answer, and probably the worst possible, is 'Because I've always wanted to.' This is alarming, because it implies that your perception of teaching originated at school and may not have been revisited, questioned or evaluated since then. It may therefore be based on a fallacious understanding of what teachers actually do.

Before you even apply for teacher training you must inform yourself about a teacher's job. It consists of much more than standing in front of groups of children, passing on knowledge. Brilliant teachers aren't just knowledgeable; they aren't just charismatic, or presentationally gifted, or good at keeping order. Hollywood versions of teaching (Whoopi Goldberg, Robin Williams) are not

to be relied on. The classroom achievements of real teachers are the tip of a range of crucial and exhausting activities, and you need to know something about those activities and how they fit together.

Of course, you should begin by examining your initial motives. There are many positive and convincing reasons for wanting to be a teacher and it will help if you prioritise these at an early stage. Here are some of the answers given typically by interview candidates. Each is a legitimate motivation but each needs to be considered for its strengths and limitations.

Because I love my subject

This is a strong and valuable motivation, especially for secondary teachers. Of course you need to know a lot about your subject, and you need to be enthusiastic about it. Indeed, children value enthusiasm in teachers very highly – more highly, in fact, than subject knowledge. The desire to kindle enthusiasm, as it was kindled in you, is a powerful and idealistic one.

On its own, however, this is not sufficient. If your prime motivation is the continued pursuit of your subject – if, for example, you see postgraduate teacher training as an alternative to master's level subject study – you are in for shocks and disappointments.

For one thing, the subject of most training courses, particularly postgraduate courses, is *education*. Subject knowledge will need extensive expansion, but this will often depend on supported self-study, while you will be formally occupied by reading, researching and understanding about children, adolescents and how they think and learn. This will include a range of professional studies as well as the study of various models of educational theory and practice. If you don't see potential fascination in this – and it is potentially fascinating, by the way, as well as creative and rewarding – then you should think again.

It's not uncommon for interview candidates to believe that teacher training is the brushing-up of presentational skills. They say, 'I know the subject, but I need to know how to get it across.' This isn't a promising starting point. Teaching is much more than 'getting it across', as we will see in later chapters. This is what makes it challenging, but it's also what makes it exciting.

In any case, your subject knowledge itself may well need considerable readjustment. Secondary English or music or maths may seem at first sight to have little to do with what you did for your degree.

And of course you were very good at it at school. This is one of the dilemmas of teaching a subject. You are (and have to be) an expert on it; but you are teaching it to people who aren't experts and who, for the most part, never will be. Many of them have little intrinsic interest in what you have to say to them. If you want to be (say) an English teacher, one of the best things to think about is the lessons you were worst at at school – not, in this case, your English lessons. In my case it was chemistry. I couldn't accept (and still don't really believe) that the world and the solid objects within it are made up of tiny revolving particles. I wasn't stupid; but I couldn't do this, however hard I tried. I couldn't understand football, either, and my team-mates used to put me in goal in the mistaken belief that there I would do least harm. I was quite large, and they told me to stand still in the hope that the ball would bounce off me. These memories are my chief allies now when I'm planning lessons – not my memories of the subjects I was good at. So you have to accept that you will be teaching your subject to pupils most of whom (statistically) don't like it. I love this; I love converting them; it beats preaching to the converted any day; but it's a complex business, and you must be aware that it's the business of every teacher, not just the unlucky ones.

Because I want to do something socially valuable

Teaching is, as we will repeatedly see, extremely hard work. Not all good teachers are idealistic, but there's no doubt that having an idealistic basis is very sustaining. When children misbehave, for example, it's enormously reassuring to remind yourself that what you're doing is important for them, of value to them rather than to you, even though they don't quite see that at the moment. All teaching should promote understanding, harmony and humanity. If you genuinely feel this, it's a good place to start. If you don't, then you should be honest with yourself and consider other aspects of the job that appeal to you instead.

This is a powerful and altruistic motivation and, like all altruism, it demands some sacrifice. Teachers' pay is better than it used to be, but it won't keep you in luxury. The workload is infinite and particularly challenging during the training period. The demands of the job are varied and unpredictable. Accountability is enormous. Social life for a trainee is extremely limited. Teachers don't finish at 3.30pm. They work in the evening and for a good part of the weekend. They do extensive preparation during the famously long holidays. These are some of the costs of your altruism.

Because I like children

Of course it's helpful if you enjoy the company of young people; children are entertaining and often hilarious. They are as varied, however, as any other group of people and you need to look straight at them rather than idealising or generalising. If you already know adolescents, you should think about how differently you might relate to them as a teacher. You may have children of your own, you may work as a teaching assistant, or in the youth service. These are valuable experiences but these relationships are not the same as those between pupils and teachers.

You are not going to be the pupils' friend in most definitions of that word. You may be closer to some of them in age than you are to your colleagues, but trading on this is at best short-lived and at worst dangerous. You will get older, but your pupils won't. And pupils like a distance between themselves and their teachers; they have friends of their own. I remember having to call my drama teacher 'Bob'. I liked drama, I liked the lessons, but I didn't want to call him 'Bob'. I liked us all to know where we were. As a trainee teacher, popularity will come easily to you. Pupils like a change and, if you're young, they will respond to that as well, for a time. You might just be able to name pop bands without looking stupid. But don't be seduced by this; it won't last. Do you really want to end up as that RE teacher who played old Beatles' songs on the guitar during those long, embarrassed assemblies? Teaching isn't a popularity contest. Doing a good job will make pupils enjoy your company and your lessons. As in other parts of life, popularity comes to those who don't go out looking for it.

Because it's creative

The process of taking what you know and causing pupils to understand its concepts and its value is certainly a creative one. Often the difference between a brilliant lesson and a mediocre one lies in relatively small adjustments. At the heart of this is the constant need to imagine the pupils' responses to what you're planning.

It's in the planning of learning that success is ensured – not, for example, in charismatic delivery. Lessons involve three elements: the teacher, the material to be taught, and the pupils. At the planning stage, only two of these will be physically present; the third – the pupils – have to be conjured up and their predicted reactions, understanding, difficulties and enthusiasms have to inform all the planning decisions that you make. Once you master this creative knack, planning starts to become easy and productive.

This need to be systematically imaginative while planning is stressful and the creativity has to be focused and informed; for example, by what you already know of the children. It is a fundamental need of planning in all secondary subjects, including those which might regard themselves as factual rather than creative. Some training teachers find this easier than others.

Furthermore, there are now major statutory policies which make detailed and compulsory statements about what we teach and how we teach it. These include the National Literacy Strategy, the National Numeracy Strategy, the National Curriculum, the Secondary Strategy and so on. You might at first be surprised to find that there is so much regulation of teaching at national level; you can look at examples of it by consulting the web sites listed in the next section. Such regulation must in some ways inhibit the personal creativity of teachers.

Gathering information

Having considered such motivations, and prioritised them for yourself, you are a step closer to answering the big question. However, as well as clarifying your own views, you need to properly inform yourself (as far as you can at this stage) about what a teacher does. You should do as much of this as you can before applying and certainly before attending for interview.

There are two main fields for this. You should read as much as you can and you should do some practical research. This research should include a formally structured school visit.

Be realistic: the personal view

In all this activity, however, you should be kind to yourself. You must always remember that you've done no training at all and are very likely to some extent to be bewildered and intimidated by what you read and see. In this and in many aspects of training you may be helped by the mostly useful 'learning-to-drive analogy'.

You may remember learning to drive. You may remember watching people using both hands and both feet while making constant and impossible decisions about steering, accelerating, not killing people, and so on. I remember thinking, 'I'll never be able to do all this'. In fact I remember my father saying (this being a long time ago, when driving instructors were considered the reckless indulgence of the very rich): 'Look at all the idiots who can drive. They all passed their test. So will you.'

The analogy works only partially. Teachers aren't idiots (I've been one for thirty years) but, nevertheless, it's encouraging to look around staffrooms and to think 'If they all got through this, so can I.' All sorts of people survive the training and do the job. But when you first begin to look at what teachers do – for example, when you first look at teachers working, or at the National Curriculum or the Standards for Qualified Teacher Status – you should expect to feel either 'I don't understand a word of this' or 'I understand it but I have no idea how to do it' or, most likely, a mixture of both. You have had no training yet. Do not be intimidated. You learned to drive; or, if you didn't, you will.

Reading and researching

This section suggests information sources which you should dip into at an early stage, while still deciding whether you want to teach, and then again early in the application process. These are materials that you will refer back to as a trainee and as a teacher and, for the most part, they aren't written directly for people in these very early stages. You cannot hope therefore to make full sense of them or to take an informed overview of them. You will notice (for example) that many formal statements about education are brief, general and abstract. This means that quite often you won't object to them – you would expect an English programme to require pupils 'to speak fluently and appropriately'; but, on reflection, you will probably conclude that it's hard to know what this actually means. How fluently? How appropriately? Appropriately to what? In whose opinion? Teachers are used to reading page after page of such material and putting it into practice. They make sense of these statements by enacting them and building a practical understanding.

You can't do that yet, although you can begin to have a look at how teachers do it (see 'The School Visit', below). You need to adopt a preliminary approach to such materials and experiences so you can begin to think about a teacher's job and also talk about your understanding at interview. My suggestion is that you adopt a *personal approach*. You cannot expect to fully appreciate the National Curriculum by reading its handbooks; but you can *select some details from it which strike you as reminiscent of your own school experiences (however long ago they were) and others which strike you as different*. This approach of *select and self-compare* will get you started.

Each section below offers a significant source, a location (usually a web site), a brief indication of content and (where appropriate) a suggestion as to the *personal approach (select and self-compare)* that you could use to begin with.

There are many useful texts – see 'Suggested Reading'. In particular, you should look at *Learning to Teach in the Secondary School* (Capel, Leask and Turner, Routledge) which offers comprehensive views of the work of a secondary teacher. Its opening chapter suggests that effective teaching is a combination of three factors – strong subject knowledge, professional knowledge and professional judgement – and makes some outline comments about what teachers actually do.

As we have already seen, teaching these days is a highly regulated activity. At the source of this regulation are various government initiatives, and you should have a look at some of their key documents and statements before you go for interview – but do remember the 'learning-to-drive' analogy and don't be overfaced by them. You may be surprised that there are so many directives and formal (even statutory) requirements behind teaching. As well as instructions, however, these bodies offer extremely rich banks of resources, many of which are helpful, ingenious and creative.

The Department for Education and Skills (http://www.dfes.gov.uk)

Has overall responsibility for schools

The Training and Development Agency for Schools (http://www.tda.gov.uk)

Is responsible for the recruitment and training of teachers and support staff; this includes initial teacher training (which is what you are currently considering) as well as subsequent training (often called 'continued professional development'). The Partners section of this web site (http://www.tda.gov.uk/partners.aspx) offers a range of useful links and a search facility which will take you to information about teachers' salaries and about training bursaries among many other things.

Select and self-compare

Check the basic entry requirements for training – do you need more qualifications? Consider the different training routes – which kind of training will suit you? Why? (See 'On the Job?' below). Look at the description of *The Teaching Week*. Is this how you expected the teacher's job to look? Does any of it surprise you? Play some of the teachers' stories in *Life as a Teacher*. Are you surprised by any of their comments? With which stories do you feel most affinity?

The Qualifications and Curriculum Authority (http://www.qca.org.uk)

Has responsibility for public examinations and qualifications. In this connection you can also look at the sites of the main public examinations bodies, which are:

AQA (http://www.qca.org.uk/)
Edexcel (http://www.edexcel.org.uk)
OCR (http://www.ocr.org.uk)
WJEC (http://www.wjec.co.uk)

Select and self-compare

Look at the *News and Updates* of the QCA web site. Choose one story that interests or surprises you. Were you aware of the QCA and of its work? Choose one of the public examinations bodies and look at its GCSE and 'A'-level specifications for your subject. Have they changed since you were at school? If so, are the changes improvements? What changes should have been made but, apparently, haven't been? How confident do you feel about your subject knowledge in terms of these specifications? What self study could you be doing to make up gaps? (Gaps are inevitable.)

The National Curriculum (http://www.nc.uk.net)

Underwrites most of the teaching in English schools. Its statements are for the most part generalised but the Key Stage 3 frameworks and the GCSE criteria offer more detailed interpretations of it.

Select and self-compare

Choose your subject and look at the appropriate programmes of study (for secondary, these are Key Stages 3 and 4). Did you study the National Curriculum when you were at school? Do you recognise your own past learning experiences in these programmes? Choose details (texts, ideas or topics) which you remember from school, and others which you don't remember. Are you confident in terms of subject knowledge? What self study could you be doing to make up gaps? (Gaps are likely.)

The Standards Site (http://www.standards.dfes.gov)

Is a DfES site which contains detailed information about the Secondary National Strategy. There are cross-curricular strategies for numeracy and literacy and frameworks for core and foundation subjects. These frameworks offer extremely detailed extensions of the National Curriculum.

Select and self-compare

Find your own subject framework. If possible, look at some of the learning objectives set out for one of the year groups (7, 8 or 9). Compare these objectives to your own school experiences and consider your own subject knowledge. Were you aware when at school of the learning objectives that lay behind your lessons? Do you think that having learning objectives at the heart of planning lessons is a good idea? Do you think the objectives listed are appropriate? How is your subject knowledge when set against these objectives?

Teachernet (http://www.teachernet.gov.uk)

Lists the Standards for Qualified Teacher Status. These will form the basis of any training course; you will have to build evidence during your training of having met them all.

Select and self-compare

Make an initial, overall response to the Standards. Is listing everything a teacher must do a sensible project, a necessity or an impossibility? Does the scope of the Standards intimidate you at this stage, or, on the other hand, do they seem reductive of the teacher's role? Consider the sections: in which areas do you feel most comfortable? In which areas would you hope for most support during training? For example, the area that causes most anxiety to prospective trainees is managing the behaviour of children. Remember that you are undertaking training so that you will be able to do these things; nobody expects you to be able to do them now, or to understand them all.

Visiting a school

You should spend as much time in a secondary school as you can before attending for interview; at least, you should visit for one day. This will help you to decide whether teaching is for you, as well as providing you with details for discussion.

Here again it's easy to be overfaced by what you see. It's helpful to take some questions with you to focus your thoughts during the visit. They might be:

- Have schools changed since you were last in one?
- Are the changes for the better?
- Are the National Curriculum and the strategies in evidence?
- How do teachers manage the behaviour of children?
- What do teachers do beyond the classroom?

- What is the atmosphere (often called the 'ethos') of the school?
- What are the attitudes of the children?

To pursue such questions you should try to arrange some specific activities for your visit. It's best to arrange these beforehand; teachers are formidably busy and will not have time to make complex arrangements on the day. Useful activities include:

Observing lessons – not just in your own subject

For example, you may ask to observe teachers who are particularly effective at behaviour management. In fact you could make behaviour management the focus of a whole day, including observations and discussions with teachers.

Pupil shadowing

Tracking a pupil's whole day is fascinating. You will follow him to break and lunch as well as to lessons. It's also exhausting – for the pupil, as well as for you. How many different concepts and activities is he involved in on a typical day? How many different teaching styles and teacher-expectation patterns does he meet? How many different kinds of behaviour are acceptable in different classrooms? Does 'silence' or 'essay' always mean the same thing? Is his day secure and predictable or varied and bewildering? Are you bored or excited by your day? How do you feel at the end of it? Is your pupil happy being followed around by a mysterious adult?

Teacher shadowing

A common question at interview is 'What do teachers do, besides teaching?' Most people know that teachers do a good deal more than standing in front of pupils, but perceptions of what this is are varied and unreliable. Even in a single day you will see your teacher marking and assessing; having very significant conversations about classes and individual pupils, often in harassed and inappropriate settings; planning lessons and assembling resources; solving crises for individual pupils; doing supervisory duties; working with a pastoral group; writing pupil reports, and so on. Of course, you should really follow your teacher home to complete the picture, but this would depend on unusually successful relationship-building during the day. Are you prepared to spend your days like this?

Meetings with teachers

Obviously you should have some key questions ready for your discussions with teachers. You can find out about the range of a teacher's workload by asking basic questions such as:

- How many classes do you teach, covering which age and ability ranges?
- How much work do you do in the evening and at weekends?
- How many non-contact periods do you have, and how do you use them?
- Do you plan lessons and work-schemes yourself, or are there shared plans already available?
- How much of your teaching is supported by learning assistants?
- Is the dreaded 'government paperwork' a substantial reality?

But you should also ask more attitudinal questions, such as:

- Is the balance of contact and non-contact time appropriate?
- Are national strategies and the National Curriculum helpful, or a hindrance?
- What should a good training course cover?
- What is the most rewarding part of the job?
- What is the most frustrating part of the job?
- Are all the stories about classroom hooligans true?
- Are exams really getting easier every year?
- What's your one best piece of advice for me?

Beware of staffrooms!

It's not uncommon for teachers to descend on trainees and berate them for even thinking about going into the profession: 'Why on earth don't you do something more rewarding/more creative/less exhausting/better paid/of higher status?' etc. It's a depressing line of questioning. It can be offered as a joke or as sincere (if cynical) advice. Many teachers do leave the profession within a short time of joining it; there are genuine issues still around the conditions

of service and the seriousness with which schools and teaching are taken. You will of course be asked about your own attitudes at interview. Meanwhile, you should reflect that staffrooms are still fairly full, and many of the teachers within them remain committed, energetic and idealistic.

Choosing a course

The TDA web site is the best place to begin when choosing a training route. There are a number of ways to achieve Qualified Teacher Status (QTS), and most routes offer additional qualifications at the same time. When looking at the range of models available, you should consider:

- your personal, domestic and financial situation;
- your preferred learning styles;
- your starting point (are you a graduate, a potential undergraduate or an experienced teacher?);
- the status of your chosen subject (especially, whether it's currently a shortage subject, which will affect financial provision).

If you are about to take a degree

You have three options:

1   You can study in your favourite subject and then complete a postgraduate teaching qualification, often a PGCE. This is the commonest route for secondary teachers, but popular also with primary teachers. There are more details below. Remember

though to choose a degree subject which will easily enable you to proceed to PGCE. If you choose to take a degree (for example) in Law you will find it difficult to find a PGCE place at the end of it.

2   You can take a B.Ed degree. In this case, your main subject will be Education, but you will study other subjects as well, and will receive QTS along with your degree. This route is popular with primary teachers.

3   You can choose a BA (QTS) or a Bsc(QTS). This is in a sense a reversal of the B.Ed degree. Here you study your chosen subject but with additional education studies, leading to QTS and a degree.

If you are a graduate

There are a number of options, and first you should consider whether you want your training to be based in a school or a university (or college); (see 'On the Job?', below). University-based training will normally take the form of a PGCE course. You should visit the web site of the Graduate Teacher Training Registry (GTTR). Look carefully at these courses. For example, an increasing number is offering master's-level credits for PGCE study. This is certainly a bonus but it's not without drawbacks. Teacher training is extremely hard work; you must think carefully about whether you want to add to those pressures.

Non-university training models for graduates include School-Centred Initial Teacher Training (SCITT) and the Graduate Teacher Programme (GTP). In both cases the training is the responsibility of the schools, though it will usually be overseen by a university. The difference is that GTP is intended for teachers who already have some experience of teaching (in independent schools, for example) whereas SCITTs are suitable for graduates new to teaching. Both of these routes will provide QTS; SCITTs will often also provide a PGCE.

On the Job?

Perhaps it will help you to consider these many and confusing acronyms if you begin with this question. Do you want your training to be university-based or school-based? There's no substantial research evidence that either makes you more employable. Head teachers of secondary schools will tend to say that they would prefer conventional university-based PGCE qualifications when choosing teachers, but they will happily appoint school-trained graduates if they consider them the best candidates at interview. So the decision really rests with you.

It's important though that this is an informed decision. The initial answer to the question often favours school-based training. It feels like a job; it may even be salaried; you are learning from those who do the work; you are spared the dreaded 'theory'. It's vital that you question these assumptions.

You must check the financial support offered for your subject in both kinds of training. In shortage subjects (and many subjects are shortage subjects) the income you will receive is broadly similar in both routes, when you take issues such as income tax and the 'golden hello' into account. Conventional PGCE trainees spend two-thirds of their time in schools; this is a practical training, and most PGCE tutors have been experienced school teachers. 'Theory' (see Chapter 4) is in fact the professional study of how children learn; proper understanding of that is clearly essential to a successful classroom.

Just as being a great mathematician doesn't necessarily make you a great maths teacher, being a great maths teacher doesn't necessarily make you a great trainer of maths teachers. On a PGCE course you will be at the centre of your tutor's concerns; on a school-based course, your tutor will have many other considerations – including, first and foremost, the progress of the children. On a university-based training, you will meet regularly with your fellow trainees and share ideas and worries with them. This peer support may be the most important advantage of conventional PGCE training.

On the other hand, school-based training works well for some people. If you are a strongly independent and organised learner, good at self-motivation and confident enough to find your own style amongst the models that surround you, school-based training may suit you better. In all training routes, trainees must become adept at evaluating their own work. This need for balanced reflection lies at the heart of progress – what went well in that lesson? what went badly? how do I build on success and what do I need to improve? This will need to be a particular strength of yours if you are to undertake school-based training.

A crucial issue here is that of integration and consistency. As we will see, trainees often run into difficulties when they perceive mixed messages coming from those around them. This will often manifest as inconsistencies between the university and the placement school. The university will demand meticulous planning; the teachers in school don't really seem to have time to do any. The university requires learning objectives for every lesson; the school teachers seem to manage perfectly well without them. They don't seem to spend hours reading theory books either.

This isn't inevitable, but it's confusing when it happens. One of the advantages that trainees report of school-based training is that (obviously) such inconsistencies are diminished; the training is homogenous. Examples given in the training are not theoretical or hypothetical, but real and drawn from the trainee's immediate environment and experiences. Problems and discoveries can be immediately analysed in a real-life and shared context. Everybody knows about that difficult Year-8 class and advice will be focused and realistic. These are strong arguments for school-based training.

However, this apparent consistency has its problems. Teaching is a very complex process. Your progress will depend upon you finding your own style, not emulating someone else's, and to do this you need to be observing, evaluating and trying as many different approaches as you can. You need a range of advice and a variety of perspectives. A danger of school-based training is that you will only experience one or two contexts, leading to a narrowing of development and a lack of versatility. There are bound to be many more approaches to teaching than those of the teachers immediately around you in school. University training gives you opportunities to reflect on the experiences of tutors, writers and your fellow-trainees and to broaden and maximise your repertoire. What can look like inconsistency may actually be the necessary reflection of the richness and diversity of teaching.

Research by the TDA indicates that trainees feel that there are positives on both sides of this argument. Trainees appear to feel that school-based training helps them to understand the teacher's job fully and to feel like a full member of staff; it is particularly supportive of behaviour-management issues, and working with other colleagues such as teaching assistants. On the other hand, trainees appear to prefer the overall quality of university-based training which they see as particularly supportive of developing subject knowledge, links between theory and practice and understanding the National Curriculum.

Having chosen between university-based and school-based training, you should consider the further options available. It's possible to undertake PGCE through School Centred Initial Teacher Training (SCITT) as well as through the conventional university route. In either case, you should now visit the web site of the GTTR (Graduate Teacher Training Registry) to look at courses and begin the application process. You should also look at the Graduate Teacher Training programme (GTP) which is a school-based system, primarily suited to people who have some experience in teaching or related work, leading to Qualified Teacher Status (QTS) but not PGCE.

You should also be aware that there are currently two types of postgraduate teaching qualification. The PGCE is a professional postgraduate qualification which includes Qualified Teacher Status (QTS). But you can also train simply for QTS on its own.

This remains confusing, so let's finally summarise the postgraduate options in the UK:

- *PGCE* is the main route and is usually a university-based one-year postgraduate course.
- *Flexible PGCE* is the same course but allows part-time working; it may also accredit previous relevant experience, leading to a shorter period of training.
- A *SCITT* is a school-based training centre which may offer PGCE or a more basic QTS course.
- The *Graduate Teacher Programme* offers school-based training leading to QTS and is particularly appropriate to people with relevant experience, some of which may be accredited.

This is all a matter of choice. The consensus among the teachers, trainees and teacher-trainers to whom I've spoken is that school-based training works well for a minority of trainees who have particular qualities and are based in schools with a particular commitment to teacher training; and that university-based training works better for the majority. Take your time choosing your training route and prepare carefully for your interview.

Chapter 2

Key journeys

Even though it's ridiculously over-used by (for example) reality-television contestants who've miraculously learned to dance, the term 'journey' is highly appropriate to the experience of trainee teachers. You will in fact undergo a number of journeys, and it's helpful to define the most significant ones and to decide how to accelerate your pace on some of them. They are set out below, and most are examined in more detail in later chapters.

Reflection on your own progress will drive your training. You need to sit down regularly and to consider where things are going well and not so well and what to do about that. Any good training course will offer supportive mechanisms for this reflection, and a useful focus for it is to consider where you are in terms of the key journeys. Use the table of continua; from time to time, mark the lines, indicating where you find yourself, and date the marks, so that you can see movement and make action plans to strengthen weaknesses and build on successes.

From you to them

I sit down with my postgraduate trainees around Christmas time; they have been training for one term, and have spent a few weeks in school. I ask them how things are going; this is part of the reflective process. Typical answers at this stage are:

- I'm still very nervous in the classroom.
- My timing and pace were all over the place, but they're beginning to improve.
- My mentor says my voice is a bit monotonous.
- I'm getting better at planning to learning objectives.
- I'm spending hours planning lessons and have no social life.

Table 2.1 Journeys – a table of continua

From	to…	and next
Teaching		*Learning*
You ————————→		Them
Activities ————→		Objectives
Extrinsic ————→		Intrinsic
Lessons ————→		Work schemes
Getting by ————→		Getting organised
Getting through it ————→		Enjoying it

- Kids are beginning to listen to me; I'm becoming more assertive.
- I'm seeing the gaps in my subject knowledge.
- There is one class I can't handle at all.
- I've not much idea of how to differentiate my teaching.
- My explanations aren't very clear.

These are perfectly legitimate responses, expressing necessary concerns, all of which can be discussed and worked on. But they are characteristic of reflection at an early stage of training. What do they have in common? What do they tend to ignore? Compare them to responses typically offered near the end of the training course:

- Kids are learning at their own pace.
- I'm more active in solving individual problems.
- I'm using more groupings in the classroom.
- Kids feel secure in asking when they don't understand.
- The plenary evaluations show me whether they've learned.
- The kids know what the learning objectives are from the start of the lesson.
- The starter lets them put the lesson into context.
- I think the transitions in the lessons signpost the learning.

These later responses are obviously more sophisticated and reflect greater experience. But the differences are more fundamental than that. The earlier responses focus on the teacher and her performance. The later responses focus on the children and their learning. This journey – from teaching to learning – is the most significant of all.

This is easy to say, but what are you to do about it? Certainly, there's no need to be embarrassed about focusing on yourself in the early stages. This is a necessary part of the process; a journey needs a starting point as well as a destination. What you can do, however, is take opportunities to focus on pupil learning as soon as you can.

For example, you should begin to consider evaluating lessons primarily in terms of what learning took place. This could apply to your observations of other teachers, as well as to your own early efforts. I remember very clearly (for example) the first lesson I ever taught, on a teaching practice, thirty years ago. The class was a low-ability Year 11 set. I stood at the front of the room and told them to do things. Astonishingly, they did them. I spoke; they listened. I asked some questions; they tried to answer them. Until that moment,

I hadn't been sure that any of this would actually happen. It was one of the most exciting moments of my life.

Naturally, like any beginning trainee, I was elated. It's perfectly fair to be delighted that you can walk into a room without falling over and talk to a class in a voice that doesn't unexpectedly rediscover puberty.

In the case of my lesson, unfortunately, nobody learned anything. The material was far too advanced and my explanations were far too sophisticated. This is normal; beginning trainees usually struggle with pitching the levels of lessons, and very often they aim too high. Over the first few weeks, you need (as I did) to begin reflecting not only on your performance, the children's behaviour and the subject content of your lesson but on what the intended learning for the lesson is, and whether this learning actually happens. In fact everything else – your materials, your subject knowledge, your planning, the clarity of your task-setting, and so on – is subservient to this. There's nothing to stop you focusing on it as soon as you start observing other teachers. What were the children meant to learn? Did they learn it? How do you know?

These three key questions will be your allies throughout your training and your teaching career. Deceptively simple, they can be employed from the outset, but in fact they go to both ends of the teaching-and-learning cycle, linking learning objectives to evaluation. When you can't answer them something is wrong with your planning. Teaching isn't performance; it isn't the 'delivery' of content (you aren't a postman); it's the creation of activity that allows learning to happen and the prime consideration in planning this is neither you nor the material, but the pupils.

From activities to objectives

The teacher was doing a web site lesson. Year 8 were designing web sites about their school. They were working in pairs; there was lots of talk and activity; some were at computers, many more were using marker pens. At first glance, it seemed to be a lively classroom.

I noticed, however, that the girls in front of me were irritated and bored; the boys beside me had spent twenty minutes writing and decorating a single word on a sheet of paper; when I quietly asked them what the web site was for, they had no idea. The apparent activity masked an essential listlessness in the room; nobody really understood what they were doing or why. On his lesson plan, in the space for *learning objective*, the teacher had written: 'to design a web site'.

Why do children need to be able to design a web site, or draw a map, or assemble a piece of apparatus? Are they going to grow up to become web site designers or cartographers? Is putting together a Bunsen burner an essential life skill? These are activities, not learning objectives. Children don't go to school to do things; they go to school to learn things.

Of course, they learn *by* doing things; but your lessons will lack purpose, focus and integrity if you don't plan them from the starting point not of what the children are going to *do*, but of what they're going to *learn*. The web site lesson might (for example) have been a lesson in thinking about a certain audience. The tone and content of a web site for prospective new pupils (for example) would be different from those of a web site for existing staff. The learning objective could have been to understand how different audiences require different presentations, different tones and different language. If the teacher had defined this for himself and focused on it in his explanations, children would have seen the point of the lesson and had something to think and talk about. Are they drawing a map in order to understand certain features of a new territory or to learn more about particular aspects of maps and how they work? Which features? Which aspects? You must start each lesson plan from these basic decisions about learning.

This all seems to me a matter of common sense, but this journey – from planning based on activities to planning based on objectives – is a difficult one for some trainees. It's a crucial journey. Trainees who reach an early understanding of it thrive, and those who don't, don't. Of course, it goes back to the three key questions – what were they mean to learn? Did they? How do I know? You can't evaluate the learning if you're not clear what the learning was meant to be. So try as soon as you can to replace 'What am I going to do?' with 'What are they going to learn?'

From extrinsic to intrinsic

We didn't like chemistry and, in fact, we suspected that Mr Smith didn't like it much either. Certainly, he didn't like it with us, because we used to wait until he went into the prep. room, and then lock him in. He used to bang feebly on the door and ask to be let out.

I'm not proud of this now, but Mr Smith was one of those teachers who was never going to be able to manage classroom behaviour. At the other end of the scale, we can all remember teachers who had immediate authority whenever they appeared. The fact is that most of us exist between these two extremes; we can manage children, but we have to work at it.

Understandably, this area of behaviour management is the most common anxiety of trainee teachers. There are many support systems in schools, and one of your earliest jobs should be to determine how your schools organise rewards and sanctions. There are also clear 'management skills' which you can practise and refine for your own use. But a significant journey involves the realisation that the best behaviour management comes from the work.

If children are misbehaving, they aren't working. If they aren't working, this can only be for one of two reasons: they can't, or they don't want to. Addressing these two possibilities is part of your planning. Is the work comprehensible and accessible? Is the level right? Are you allowing a range of approaches to suit different ways of learning? Are your explanations clear? Do you start from where the pupils are, rather than from where you are? Are you explaining the point and purpose of what's going on? Brilliant trainees (and teachers) come to understand that good lesson planning will eradicate most bad behaviour, and that poor planning will guarantee it. We will examine these issues in detail in Chapter 6. But as soon as you can you should be trying to reflect on good and bad behaviour in terms which include re-examining your lesson plans as well as seeking advice on behaviour-management skills.

From lessons to work schemes

Planning is the most important thing a teacher does. More than subject expertise or charismatic delivery, good planning underpins security in the classroom, continuity of learning and, incidentally, good behaviour.

In the early stages, planning takes up an enormous amount of time, and this disproportionality will rectify itself as your training progresses. It's not unusual for a beginning trainee to take six hours to plan a twenty-minute lesson segment – and she may be working with a friend. Don't panic – this will (and must!) change.

We will consider planning in detail in Chapter 5, but it's helpful now to record that a key movement is from planning individual lessons to seeing those lessons as parts of sequences, often known as work schemes or medium- (or long- or short-) term plans. The effectiveness of teaching in fact lies not in brilliant lessons but in lessons which fit together to generate learning through range and reinforcement. This may sound daunting at the outset, though in fact 'planning backwards' – beginning with broader considerations rather than starting with lesson one – is in many ways easier. You won't be in a position to do this from the outset but you can adopt certain routines to help you build this perspective. When observing other teachers, for example, you should ask about the work scheme and how the lesson fits into it, rather than just considering the lesson itself. They fit together in terms of learning objectives, so you should be trying to understand how the lesson objectives are married to the work-scheme objectives to create a journey for the pupils. At the early stages, you probably won't be able to plan like this, but you can certainly watch for it in the work of experienced colleagues. And even in your early, fledgling planning, you should always be thinking of the lesson before and the lesson after the one you're actually working on.

From getting by to getting organised

A couple of years ago, when asked what event had been most significant in her training, one of my students wrote 'I bought a filing cabinet.' The work of a teacher is immensely complex and varied. You are a factory worker, a trainer, a bureaucrat and an executive manager. In any other walk of life you would do only one of these jobs, and in most of them you would have other people helping you. The sheer size and diversity of the teacher's role is exhausting. It imposes formidable organisational demands and the sooner you accept this and do something about it, the better.

This isn't so bad if you're a naturally organised person. You will have a portable filing-case, you will build cross-referenced banks of resources, you will colour-code your timetable and your different classes, you will print your lesson plans on coloured paper (easier to find on your desk mid-lesson), you will begin with an elaborate mark-records book, you will always know who attended your lessons (someone might ask), you will have printed back-ups in case PowerPoint lets you down (it usually does), you will allocate on your timetable specific marking and preparation tasks as well as lesson times.

Many people, however, don't take this on in the early stages. It took me a year or two before I realised, finally, that it isn't romantic to be a charismatic maverick, loved by the pupils even as you lose their homework, brilliant 'in the classroom' but largely incapable of preparing for or tracking their progress, irritated by the so-called 'efficiency' of the other, older, boring teachers. This set of attitudes isn't uncommon in trainees, but it needs to be abandoned, because it will end in tears. Being organised isn't only an essential professional courtesy, it is necessary to make your own life as a teacher sustainable. If it doesn't come naturally, you have to consciously devise explicit systems for it. The less organised you are, the more organised you have to be. This is a matter of survival.

Chapter 3

Being a teacher

It's often good practice to show children models of what they're trying to achieve. How do you write an 'essay' when no one has ever shown you what an essay actually is? As a trainee, you will have a model of what a teacher looks like and this image of the finished product is an important motivator and reference point for you. However, it will change as you train. Having a sense of where your model comes from and how and why it's developing will help your reflection and progress.

When I was at school ...

Many of us begin training because we were well taught at school. We carry images of good teaching, often from our own subject areas. We are aware of the influence of these powerful figures and, quite legitimately, we seek to have similar influence. We seek to inspire, as we were inspired.

Why does this image have to change and develop? It's helpful to think of its particular contextual limitations. For one thing, imitating a charismatic individual will not make you charismatic. This is a personal quality and comes from within. As your training proceeds you will find those qualities within you which, when organised, amplified and deployed, will make you an effective practitioner. Of course, all of professional life is a kind of role-playing; I don't talk to my wife in the way I talk to my students; but children have an instinctive sense of integrity; they can tell when you're playing a part which proceeds from outside rather than inside, and they will not respect this. I often watch trainees begin their classroom lives with a full set of mannerisms based on their own favourite teachers. These stabilisers may be useful for the first few weeks but they become increasingly irrelevant.

To help you with this kind of journey it's useful at an early stage to make a list of personal qualities which may eventually find their ways into your classroom. Consider whether you're patient, well organised, generous, a good listener, humorous, energetic, calm, fair-minded, enthusiastic, a good starter, a good finisher, good on detail, good on overview, talkative, reserved, predictable, unpredictable and so on. Any sub-set of such qualities can begin to form your teaching persona.

There are other limitations to the *favourite teacher* model. You only saw your favourite teacher working in a certain classroom, from the viewpoint of pupils of whom at least one (and probably more) loved the subject. I frequently see trainees bewildered when their initial classroom efforts, based on the kind of vigorous whole-class questioning that their own teachers used, fall on deaf ears. What worked on you won't necessarily work on everybody.

And, finally, it has to be said that requirements placed on teachers, and the attitudes that accompany them, have changed. Teaching (as required, for example, by the Secondary Strategy) is much more commonly interactive and varied than it used to be. Being lively at the front of the room is no longer enough – if, indeed, it ever was.

Observing teachers – the importance of comparison

The building of your sense of teacher-self will be greatly enhanced by observing other teachers; this is discussed briefly in Chapter 1 and again in Chapter 4. This is a more reliable and immediate source of information than the *favourite-teacher* model or the wholly unreliable *Hollywood-charismatic* model where maverick unconventionality is the key to immediate and astonishing success. Observing real teachers will be a compulsory part of your training, though often only at the beginning, which is regrettable, since it is actually very powerful for experienced trainees as well.

Any training course will offer you instruments to support your observation of teachers, encouraging you to chart pupil activity and relate it to teacher activity, to consider learning objectives, behaviour-management techniques and so on. It's important though to be clear about why you're doing this.

It's very helpful to have a focus for observation. For example, you may be struggling with the behaviour of your Year-9 class. Your mentor will arrange for you to see a Year-9 class being taught by someone who is particularly effective in this area. What are you supposed to make of this? It's absolutely central to your development that this kind of process works for you, and it will only work if all concerned understand what all this activity is for. It's not for you to observe, learn and emulate. Teacher training isn't an apprenticeship. As we've already said, what works for that teacher may well not work for you. So why are you watching him?

You're watching him to enhance your own reflection. *What matters, then, is not the observation itself but the evaluation, reflection and discussion which it provokes.* Your mentor in school needs to understand that this has practical implications. What you have to do is consider the distinct qualities of that teacher. *This is a process of comparison.*

Of course, the most significant comparison is with your own practice. The teacher makes the pupils line up outside the classroom and reminds them about behaviour routines before he allows them in. This looks like a good idea; you don't do it, and your own lesson beginnings are bordering on the horrific. So you make a note, and next time, you attempt to line up your own Year 9 in the same way. One of them swears at you and three go to the toilet. So what have you got out of the observation?

Without reflection, you've got very little. Reflection depends on discussion and comparison. Discussion here would take you not just to simple replication of a technique but to proper analysis of what the teacher has and you don't. For example, he clearly understands the significance of *beginnings*; behaviour is more easily settled then than later. He clearly understands and uses various classroom *routines*. He also understands that pupils need to be regularly *reminded* of those routines – this is a routine in itself. So he has three things to offer you.

By reflecting on these three areas – beginnings, routines and communication – you might then begin to devise some new approaches of your own. For example you might think again about starter activities (beginnings), about what your key classroom rules are (routines), about making a poster of your three key rules (communication). Discussion has turned the observation data into a source for your reflection and development. You don't copy it, but you learn from it.

How does this happen? Observation should not be organised in your school without the formal opportunity for you to discuss what you've observed. You should have time to discuss the lesson both with the teacher observed and with your mentor. Observation without proper discussion, especially in the early stages, is almost pointless, and can even be damaging.

We have said the comparison is at the heart of this process, and that the fundamental and inevitable comparison is between the observed practice and your own. This reflective process can be greatly enhanced, however, by observing two teachers with the same observation focus. One of them lines the children up and talks to them quite firmly; the other lets them wander in as they please and chats to them abut their lives and worries in a surprisingly informal way. Seeing both of these lesson beginnings is far more than twice as good as seeing only one in terms of the kind of discussion and personal reflection that this is likely to provoke. You should always try to arrange observations in pairs and then to think about which way your own practice might be going. Which model attracts you? What are the limitations of both? Which reminds you more of your own practice? Are they in fact as different as they look?

Jenny – a teacher's day

Jenny is in her second year of science teaching and has no particular formal responsibility post. A typical working day is as follows:

8.45am   Staff briefing: All staff take notes of announcements and issues concerning the pupils and the school day. Jenny takes notes particularly regarding her pastoral group.

9.00   Pastoral group: Collect and take attendance register for group. Give notices. Collect absence notes and file. Collect raffle tickets and money. Remind pupils about absence notes, trips, raffle tickets. Talk to one pupil about homework complaints from other staff. Work with group on preparation for assembly which group is taking next week; this concerns bullying, which is a PHSE theme for the half term; the group will present a piece of improvised drama.

9.15   Teaching Year 9

10.15   Non-contact period: Checking in Year 9's homework from previous lesson. Starting to mark it. Seeing lab technician regarding next lesson. Seeing pastoral head regarding one problem in the tutor group. Checking lesson notes for next lesson.

11.15   Break: Continue above activities and try to have coffee.

11.30   Teaching Year 12

12.30pm   Lunch: Department meeting regarding new 'A'-level topics. Check lab for afternoon lessons.

1.30   Teaching Year 8

2.30   Teaching Year 7

4.00   Twilight training session: Tracking pupil progress.

Evening   Complete Year 9 marking, begin Year 7 marking. Prepare Year 12 topic for tomorrow – reading and planning. Look at new exemplar Year 12 assessment scripts from examination board.

Teachers do manage this workload, with its range of *academic*, *administrative* and *pastoral* tasks. You may be overfaced by it in the early stages, and trainees are often concerned that they are exhausted even though they have a fraction of a real teacher's timetable. It's common to ask 'If I can't manage now, how on earth will I manage when I've got to do twice as much?'

You will manage it. Remember that as a trainee you have things to do that teachers don't; and, of course, it's all new to you. With a little experience, gargantuan tasks become routine and even trivial, and this shrinkage will probably begin before you complete the training. Finishing trainees are often amazed by the progress they've made in this area as in others. Meanwhile, just remember that managing the workload is an activity in itself. Being a professional (more below) means that you have to take seriously all three elements of the job; it's not acceptable or sustainable to shine at one of them at the expense of the others. So you should divide your time among them; use your timetable document to mark up administrative and pastoral routines as well as taught lessons.

You should try to be realistic about all this. Planning is the solution to workload problems. Saying you haven't got time to plan is like the man who, having bought a large round of drinks, is offered a tray by the barman. 'A tray?' says the customer. 'No thanks. I've got enough to carry!'

For example, the marking load can seem ridiculous in the early stages. Teachers learn to stagger their homework setting so that three batches of marking don't appear at the same time. They learn that not all homework needs to be written. They also use a range of assessment techniques such as peer assessment (see Chapter 8) which are valid in themselves and which spread the workload a little. A little forward thinking removes bottlenecks. Planning well is being kind to yourself.

In particular, you should formally plan your non-contact periods. You should allocate marking, planning or study tasks to them in advance so that they don't just become 'free' periods where you drink coffee and stare into space. You should also decide where after-school work is going to go. Some teachers take it home, others stay in school every day until 6pm. You need to trial and develop a system; if you don't run the workload, the workload will run you.

I'm a professional ...

Student teacher is an interesting term. It isn't an oxymoron; all good teachers are also learners; the best lessons are those where the teacher learns something as well as the pupils. As a trainee, you should make the most of the symbiosis. Being a learner provides you with many opportunities to reflect on learning from the learner's point of view. Which lectures, seminars, tutors, mentors, teachers, experiences, activities and readings are consistently beneficial to you? Which are not beneficial? Why? Brilliant teachers plan and teach with a clear sense of the experiences of learners, and your position as learner-teacher provides rich reflection data to support this process.

When you are in school, however, you have to be clear that you are a *teacher*, not a *student*. This sense of professionalism informs every aspect of your work, from the outset of the training. Teachers place a high value on professionalism, and you will be judged on it regularly. It's a grand and over-used concept, so it's helpful to define it in practical terms.

Why do teachers prize concepts such as professionalism and 'efficiency' so highly? Why does all this matter? Surely it's being terrific in the classroom that counts? Professionalism has to do with being a member of a profession. Based as it therefore is on membership, it's essentially bound up with convention and conformity; clubs have rules. This may at times feel irksome (especially to those still locked into the maverick-genius model) but it's inevitable. One aspect of this membership is that you are working in complex institutions which cannot survive without agreed ethical codes of behaviour and relationships. Another is that you agree to be committed to the work and to your own professional development – for example, to the willing and sustained development of your subject knowledge and pedagogy. Beyond this, teachers are committed to the well-being of their pupils and the schools they work in. For example, in the United Kingdom they are committed to the principles of the *Every Child Matters* initiative (www.everychildmatters.gov.uk) and to other national and institutional policies. The national and local behaviours and concerns that constitute professionalism underpin processes that make schools work for the good of children. There's therefore a direct logical link between doing your best for the kids and behaving professionally. This doesn't mean (of course) that as a teacher you must lose your creative individuality.

These thoughts about professionalism remain rather abstract, so we should consider how teachers define professionalism in themselves. These are some of the things that teachers do; failure to do them can appear as unprofessional behaviour. As requirements, they apply absolutely to you as a trainee as well as later.

They present themselves appropriately

At school, you dress as a teacher from day one. This will help you to feel like a member of staff and will enhance your status in the eyes of the pupils.

They work to deadlines

Schools are running deadlines all the time. You may be used to negotiating the odd extra few days for the submission of an assignment, but in schools the failure to meet a deadline will compromise many other people. Completing a set of pupil reports, for example, is only one stage of a complex process which will include further completion, record-taking, checking, modification and distribution. Of course, if you are having difficulties, you should talk to colleagues about them; but regular failure to meet deadlines will be regarded as a professional issue.

They learn and use the school's systems

As early as possible, you should come to understand key school policies – for example, those surrounding behaviour management. You're not a slave to these policies but they can be of enormous benefit and, as a professional, you should be seen to be using them. This extends to your subject work; should you be writing learning objectives on the board before each lesson? How does your own lesson planning relate to the department's schemes of work?

They make themselves available

Unbelievably, teacher-training candidates at interview quite frequently say that they want to be teachers because they have children and the hours will be convenient for them. This is a spectacularly poor answer for a number of reasons, one of which is that it isn't true. Teachers expect to work after school, during their breaks and at the weekend. As a trainee you should expect to attend meetings during lunch hours and at the end of the day; some of these will be informal and arranged with little notice. Of course you can't do the impossible, but you should add at least half-an-hour to the school day before you consider going home.

They make appropriate relationships with pupils

This is an enormous area and we will consider it in more detail in later chapters. The one consideration that will always guide you in the right direction is that this is *a working relationship*. You aren't there to be the pupils' friend or champion; popularity is not of itself your goal; your job is not to perform excitingly but to create environments in which learning takes place. Once this becomes your focus, it isn't so hard to achieve. Well-chosen material, clear learning objectives, appropriate activities and a consistent classroom manner will help to generate an atmosphere of collaboration. These matters are discussed in detail in Chapters 4, 5 and 6.

What you have to get right (and it takes time) is the matter of *the space between you and them*. There has to be a space for the relationship to work, because it's in this space that the learning happens; don't trample over it. It has to be clearly defined. It can change size, but only in one direction. It can grow smaller as you get to know them; you can gradually approach them over a period of time; but you can't make the space bigger. You can't retreat. So start at a little distance and let the relationship grow.

To be more direct, what is potentially *unprofessional* in this area? Trainees are often tempted to seek initial popularity by being over-familiar, cracking jokes, appearing slightly 'mould-breaking'. It's understandable; gaining the pupils' attention and co-operation is a major concern in the early stages, and this can seem a shortcut to success. It's not sustainable, however; it's almost certain to turn round and bite you within a few weeks. When they misbehave (they do, they will) where does such a teacher go? There is ancient wisdom about this: *firm-and-friendly* and *don't smile until Christmas* aren't bad mantras, though I wouldn't be absolutely literal about the smiling. Hold something back; let the pupils discover you over a period of time.

Use appropriate language. Attempts at youth slang may have some short-term success (if you're young enough to carry it off) but in the end it won't help to build the small but important distance that needs to be between you and them. Swearing, even mild swearing, is never acceptable, even though the pupils (of course) know all the swear words (including some you don't) and are unlikely to be corrupted by hearing them. In such areas, it might help to imagine pupils describing your teaching to their parents when they go home.

This doesn't mean that you should be unfriendly, but the friendship should be generalised; you should look as though you like being there and doing the job. You should avoid anything that can seem like individual friendship or favouritism (and this can be difficult, some children are very needy). If a pupil wants to confide in you (it's not uncommon with trainee teachers) you should seek immediate guidance from colleagues in school. You should avoid being alone with individual pupils in private spaces (for example, empty classrooms, especially with closed doors). You should never, for any reason, touch a pupil. You should never discuss colleagues with individuals or with groups of pupils. It can feel good to be told (probably quite sincerely) that you're a much better teacher than Mr Ellis, but this conversation absolutely cannot even begin to happen. Close down any such overture by reminding pupils that there is work to be done. Similarly, don't discuss school policies or rules with pupils unless this is part of a properly planned activity which (therefore) your mentor has already discussed and cleared with you.

They make appropriate relationships with colleagues

Your relationship with your mentor is crucial to your training. It's a complex relationship, combining support with assessment, and we will examine it in Chapter 4. For the moment, it's important to remember that professional courtesy and tact are at the heart of it. This relationship is a machine which runs every day; professionalism is the lubrication that lets this happen.

That's not to say that you shouldn't be assertive when it's appropriate, but remember that, even if you disagree with her at times, your mentor knows more about teaching than you do. You should seek always to understand her observations about your teaching and to use them as part of your reflection. Defensiveness is not uncommon in trainees who feel that they're being criticised; though understandable, it's almost always a barrier to progress. Before you even begin training, you should think about how well or badly you react to criticism.

We have to be clear though that, in working relationships, professionalism isn't a euphemism for keeping your mouth shut when you're unhappy. On the contrary, the professional approach is to actively raise issues of concern, positively, in the right way, with the right people. If you genuinely think that your mentor's behaviour is unreasonable, you should seek to discuss this, initially, with her rather than anybody else. Assertiveness is a professional necessity.

Similar routine courtesy applies to your dealings with all staff. Professionalism is shown by understanding and using the proper communications channels, especially when raising contentious issues; by finding positive ways to address difficulties; by being reliable in your dealings with people. Ranting about a colleague in a corner of the staffroom, for example, is not professional.

They carry out their responsibilities

Being three minutes late for a lecture might earn you a quizzical look. If you are late for a lesson, a pupil may have broken a window or his arm in those three minutes and, as a teacher, you are responsible for that. Working with children imposes a range of legal and ethical responsibilities. You should learn what these are and, even though as a student teacher you do not (and cannot) carry them, you will be expected to behave in schools exactly as though you did. So what might at first seem irksome or petty issues of timekeeping are vitally important in the running of schools and in your professional behaviour.

What will be considered professional here? If you are ill you must notify the school (probably before 8:30am) and set work for classes. If you have a meeting with a colleague you must attend it and bring all the paperwork; saying 'Oh, sorry, I left it at home', won't do. If you are required to, you must show your work-scheme and lesson planning to your mentor according to deadlines. If you are struggling to meet such deadlines, you should discuss the difficulties in advance. If you can't get your marking done in a timely fashion, you should ask your mentor for support and guidance well before it's due. Professionalism is about heading off crises.

Attendance can be an issue for trainee teachers. I'm quite regularly asked by trainees if they can miss school (or university) time for reasons such as a childcare problem, a dental appointment or a visit from a relative who lives abroad. You should talk to teachers about what time they take off and what for; permissions are few and far between and, except in genuine emergencies, reasons such as these would not be entertained. You may find this to be quite a different culture to what you've been used to. Nobody is trying to be unhelpful but if you miss time, someone else has to make it up for you. Year 8 can't simply be left in a pile on your desk until you return. Nor can they be left to their own devices without an adult in the room.

But I want to be myself ...

This may all seem rather daunting, especially if the teachers we remember from our childhoods are the eccentric, flamboyant, unconventional ones. Is there space for individuality within this professional world?

Professionalism provides a place where your personality can grow; it provides the banks without which, as the poet said, there is no river. This relationship between structures and spontaneity in fact underpins most good teaching. In the classroom, clear structures provide the security within which children can experiment and discover. Within your own development, professionalism contributes to the framework which contains your classroom persona. It's a commonplace that we all inhabit differing personas as we go through the day – mother-persona, wife-persona, meeting-with-bank-manager-persona; these take us to different versions of ourselves, with different behaviours and different languages. Some are more customary and natural to us than others, but they all proceed from us and provide toolkits for the various roles which life requires of us. So we should accept that we are building a teacher-persona without feeling that this is an essential betrayal. The persona will come, and it may not be the one you expected, but it will only work if it is an authentic version of yourself.

Chapter 4

Being a trainee

Being a trainee isn't just being a junior teacher. There are things that you have to do that teachers don't, and vice versa; there are particular advantages, challenges and pressures. In this chapter we will consider the difficulties and opportunities of this complex and sometimes confusing role.

Pressure points – Don't panic!

There are predictable points of stress within a training course. You are learning difficult crafts in a highly-charged and (at times) judgmental environment. Changing jobs is stressful, and in most training courses you do this about three times.

Changing to a new placement, for example, can often generate a bout of depression. On PGCE courses this often happens in the new year; the February plateau is well documented. Having worked hard to get a sense of how you can function in your first school you are suddenly parachuted into another and everything you thought you'd learned now seems irrelevant. Instead of moving forward, you seem to be moving back. These are the dark days of teacher training. So what do you do?

First of all, accept it as a reality of the training, not as a personal failure. Recognise that most of your fellow-trainees are going through it as well. I field many lengthy telephone conversations at these times and trainees often ask whether they're alone in their predicaments. They aren't.

Second, then, you need to talk to somebody. Your peers (though some may be good at hiding it) are feeling what you're feeling. Because these difficult periods are so well known that there's actually published research about them, your tutors and mentors will also be able to reassure you. Raising small, early problems is always better than being swamped later on. Trainees who don't raise problems or don't appear to have any are the ones who worry me.

Be kind to yourself

You're allowed to have off-days and bad lessons. Take the matter of lesson evaluations, for example. You are probably required to evaluate your own teaching – if you aren't, you should be. You should ask the three key questions – 'What were they meant to learn? Did they learn it? How do I know?' – at the end of every lesson. But often, in such an evaluative conversation, trainees are excessively negative. They are their own severest critics. When asked, 'How do you think it went?' they will list every poor feature of the lesson. Just as your mentor should routinely address positives as well as weaknesses in her feedback, so should you *make it a rule to find the good points of the lesson*. This doesn't always come naturally, but it's extremely unlikely that the lesson had no virtues of any kind. It was dull, but they behaved themselves. Or, they behaved appallingly, but the lesson demonstrated your good subject knowledge. The main activity was too challenging but the starter was appropriate. Force yourself to be positive.

Set yourself realistic targets

Any good training course will have a central target-setting regime. In conjunction with your mentor, you should set development targets over relatively short timespans and *you should monitor your progress and success*. For example, you could set targets over a week. Here's a useful cycle:

Observation

Your mentor watches you teach. She observes, among other things, that your questioning technique is limited and needs expanding. Asking a range of question types is essential to good teaching and this will be discussed in later chapters. For example, some questions – sometimes called closed or convergent questions – have right answers, while others are open to opinion – often called open or divergent questions. Having both types in a lesson is part of its essential variety; you are trying to appeal to a range of different people with different learning styles. But your mentor has noticed that you don't ask many open questions.

Discussion

The next stage is to discuss this observation, perhaps as part of the lesson feedback. Your mentor will explain the point and you will understand it. *Very often, this is where the process ends.* This and a number of other 'weaknesses' in your practice have been raised. You soldier on; each week, a few more problem areas are added to the list. In fact any teacher could watch any other teacher throughout infinity and never stop finding things that could be better. That's the nature of the job.

It's not surprising if this becomes depressing. *This isn't your fault; it's because the process isn't working.* You must take charge of it (if necessary) to ensure that it doesn't stop at this point but continues to its positive conclusion. So, to continue:

At this *discussion* stage, you consider which lessons next week might offer opportunities to expand your questioning technique. You discuss a few possible example questions that you might ask. This may be one of two or three targets for the week.

Note before we go on how *specific* this target is. Generalised targets are close to useless. 'Improve behaviour management' is a useless target. How do you do that, then? 'Settle classes at lesson beginnings' is much better. This is equally true of pupils' learning objectives; make them few, small and local. Big objectives may sound grand, but they don't tell you what to do on Thursday morning.

So, after *discussion*, you understand this point about questioning, and you have some idea of what you're going to do about it.

Lesson planning

Next week, you consider where to try out this expanded questioning. It doesn't just relate to the observed class. Your Year 10 is doing some work on climate change; you could involve them in some opinion-base questioning. Your Year 8 could also offer some opinions on environmental tourism. So that target is now being enacted in your planning.

At this stage it's a very good idea to indicate on your lesson plan that you have this particular target for yourself (as well as objectives for the pupils) in this lesson. Your mentor, when she watches the lesson, will have this focus particularly in mind because she has your lesson plan in front of her.

Observation again

So, now your mentor, watching your lesson, will comment in her feedback on your progress with questioning. She may feel you've done very well and can move on to other targets arising from the observation; or she may feel you need to work more on it.

Discussion again

In the discussion of the lesson, you will agree on your progress with questioning.

Let's summarise this simple process:

*   lesson observation sets targets;
*   discussion defines targets;
*   lesson planning selects targets;
*   observation focuses on targets;
*   discussion evaluates targets.

This is a process which works against the sometimes overfacing feeling that there's far too much to learn and you can't do anything right. It's successful because:

*   the targets are few (no more than three in a week);
*   the targets are specific;
*   the targets are discussed and agreed;
*   there's discussion of how to enact the targets;
*   you decide where to place the targets in your planning;
*   the timespan is small, so you can hold the process in your head;
*   the targets aren't just left to drift, but are evaluated, giving you a sense of progress and achievement.

There are in fact some *key principles* here that should underpin all of your training and carry you through difficult times. One is that you should *always try to work with specifics*. Large, general issues and concerns need to be broken down into local, specific actions. Specific objectives (for children and for you) are handrails to hold onto on a confusing and sometimes precarious journey.

Another key principle is that significant processes will only work to support you if they are fully understood and completed by all concerned – and this includes your mentors as well as yourself. For example, we have been talking about the need to evaluate lessons and the need to set targets. These are clearly connected processes, but each needs to be fully worked through. They key principle here is that *very often you must take charge*. If the processes aren't working, it may well be your job to discuss with your mentor how things could be improved. This may be a difficult conversation to have, but it will be highly beneficial. We will come to it again later in this chapter.

How else can you ward off depression? Planning matters – depression and fatigue are certainly connected and, as we've repeated to the point of tedium, planning averts bottlenecks. There are other good reasons for careful planning. Sometimes the stress factor is simply the workload. Trainees with experience in industry or other public services (even including nursing) claim teacher training to be very hard work indeed; so, up to a point, you have to accept the workload and organise around it. But sometimes that point is reached and exceeded. Your mentor, for example, hands you 100 Year 9 SATs papers to mark. You are overwhelmed by this; depression, tinged with anger and self-doubt, sets in. You have no idea of how or when you are going to do this work.

Why has your mentor done this to you? You may suspect that she's offloading her own work but it's much more likely that she intends you to experience the stresses and commitments that teachers have to live with. The first thing to say about such a situation is that there may be a misconception here about the nature of your placement. You aren't on work experience or job sampling; you are being trained. Activities should be training activities, and this means that you don't have to do everything that teachers do. You don't really have to do break duty, or cover for absent colleagues, or invigilate exams. The criterion isn't *teachers do it, so you should, too*. The criterion is *this is a training opportunity*. Against that criterion, I would argue that co-marking ten of the SATs papers and discussing them and the assessment criteria is a much higher-value training activity than marking all of them in your back bedroom. So you may have to have a difficult conversation with your mentor (see below). What will help in any such conversation is that you can show a detailed planning document which includes a timetable not only of your classes but of specific marking and planning for specific groups, specific administrative and pastoral task allocation, and specific university assignment times as well. You are showing that you are organised and professional; and you are showing that your time is already overloaded. Planning puts you in a stronger negotiating position.

A further word on forward planning. Don't underestimate how relieving it is to have scheduled those tasks that have been hanging over you. No, you haven't started your research project yet; but you know that you're going to start it a week on Tuesday. Even (or perhaps especially) if you're not a natural list-maker, the making of lists can be a great lifter of pressure.

Include personal time (Friday nights?) in your plan. Meet with peers and laugh. Alcohol is, in fact, available on prescription to trainee teachers. (This isn't true but I thought it might cheer you up.) Make a point of dwelling on (even writing down) moments of real contact with children. It's a common feature of classrooms that the teacher's attention is held by one or two naughty children. This is disproportionate, and (of course) a behaviour-management issue; but you mustn't allow this imbalance to creep into your wider reflections. Three girls were objectionable but fourteen others were getting something from you; two of them were almost excited. You must force yourself not just to think about the three problems. The penny dropping for one Year-8 boy half-way through a ragged lesson is a key moment for him and for you. That's why you're there and that's what you have to hang on to.

Peer support

There are many exciting moments during training, when you re-connect with wanting to be a teacher, when the pieces start to drop into place. In the darker times, however, one of your trump cards is peer support. Your fellow trainees will help you out with morale-boosting techniques and lesson ideas and share the February blues with you; a kind of blitz spirit emerges and you will certainly make some life-long friends.

One of the problems with this rosy picture, however, is that you may well spend most of your training working in a school miles away from any other trainees. University sessions may enable you to

meet from time to time, and you may have a regular Friday drinking session on your timetable; but how do you ask whether anybody has any ideas about the excitement of right-angled triangles or how to ban competitive burping in Year 8?

One simple solution is the internet. Trainees who have regular access to a group emailing list say that it's a lifeline. Your trainers may provide such a list, but if they don't, or if you want a more informal or private communication, you could set up your own. There are several internet providers of such services; they are free and easy to set up and run. Visit http://groups.yahoo.com; you can set up a group in about twenty minutes. The group allows the exchange of emails (a single email sent to the group is automatically sent to every member); the addition of web links (there are hundreds of educational web sites listed on my own group); and, very usefully, the storage of files – my own group site holds many lesson-planning documents. If you visit http://groups.yahoo.com/group/pgceenglish you can have a look at how trainees use it.

Taking control

Sue phones me. She's unhappy; her mentor never seems to say anything positive about her teaching. Feedback is friendly but restricted to lengthy accounts of how the lesson could be improved. After five weeks of this, Sue is demoralised. She thinks the mentor has no confidence in her, and she is losing confidence in herself.

This situation is, in fact, extremely common. Why is the mentor being so negative? Usually, it's not a sign of concern or of a belief that the trainee is useless. Usually, the mentor has no idea that he is having such a depressing effect. He is simply trying to do his job. In fact the detailed criticism results from the opinion that Sue is rather good, and worth spending time on. If she can listen to his advice, Sue will progress and will finish the placement with a high rating. Tips on how to improve, the mentor thinks, are the quickest way to success.

On such an occasion, I offer some alternatives. I could speak to the mentor about Sue's progress; I could suggest a more positive approach to feedback. I could suggest that he attempts always to offer praise as well as criticism. Mentors are sometimes astonished by this; they're used to praising children, and know all about self-worth and achievement, but they forget about this when dealing with other adults. They can forget how vulnerable you are within that relationship.

I can tactfully remind the mentor of this on Sue's behalf, but I usually offer a different (and better route): that Sue take it up

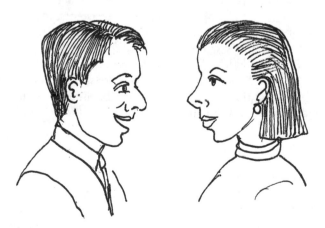

herself. She agrees to raise this with the mentor. A week later, I phone her. Things are fine now, she says, seeming a little surprised that I've bothered to call.

This pattern is repeated over and over again. If you have issues with colleagues, be pro-active. Consider whether and how you can raise them properly and professionally yourself. Remember that teachers are very busy and that you aren't their top priority. This means that they may be occasionally careless with you but it doesn't mean that they don't want to do their best. They aren't mind readers. Schedule a meeting with your mentor and take some control of the agenda.

This is equally true of seeking support with issues of your teaching. The most important aspect of your professional development is communication. A common character on training courses is the student teacher who won't admit to classroom problems. Year 9 is going badly wrong but David doesn't want to discuss it; he wants to sort it out for himself. This is absolutely understandable; he wants to prove to himself and to others that he can handle things. He's aware that the very person he must approach for help is the person who will decide whether he should pass or fail in a few weeks' time. So he soldiers on; and things go from bad to worse.

This common scenario is suicidal. If things are going wrong, you must seek support at an early stage. You are a trainee; nobody expects you to be able to do everything. The longer you allow it go on, the more difficult the situation will be to resolve. Your mentors are impressed by professional behaviour, and professionals seek support. The children in that Year-9 class deserve proper teaching. And the situation is unsustainable, because in fact your mentors already know what's happening and will insist on intervening, at which point you've had control taken away from you.

One of my trainees wrote, 'They say that you learn from your mistakes. It's a good idea, then, to make as many mistakes as possible in the early stages.' Getting things wrong doesn't matter. Everyone expects you to get things wrong. You won't be judged on that; you'll be judged on what you do about it.

You and your mentor

No one is more significant to your training than your school mentor. This is a vital and complex relationship and you have to work at it. At the heart of its complexity is its combination of support and assessment. Your mentor wants to encourage you.

She wants you to feel secure and free to raise issues. She wants above all to build your confidence, especially in the early stages. At the same time, she owes it you to raise problems with you when she sees them; if they were never addressed, she may even be making future decisions about whether your training continues or not. Combining these two roles is very challenging and it's not uncommon for this to lead to delays in facing up to issues. A mentor spots problems in your practice; she decides that it's too early to mention them without damaging your confidence; you are aware that things aren't perfect but hope they'll get better; and the situation drifts. The problems get worse, and you're left feeling unclear as to what they are or how to address them. This isn't a book for mentors, but if it were, I'd write: raise the issues early. The instinct to leave them is a generous and understandable one, but in practice it leads to deterioration.

Training is an individual business; your responses to your mentoring are to some extent unknown and unpredictable so, as we said earlier, you may need to take control. If things aren't right, you must raise this. The duality of the role and the relationship place particular pressures on you in beginning any such conversation; but such conversations may need to be had.

Remember that your mentor is a teacher. In broaching issues – either of your teaching, or even of her mentoring – you should bear in mind a couple of features of her job which can influence this relationship. They are: *teachers don't like to be wrong; but they do very much like to help.*

Teaching can be a lonely job. Your mentor (like all teachers) spends her life in a classroom without much adult support. She is surrounded by adolescents who make constant demands on her. These demands may include requests for unexpected and unplanned subject information, poor behaviour which challenges her authority, the need to rethink and reorganise the lesson, and so on. In the middle of all this, the teacher has to remain authoritative. It's her job to have the right answers; her opinions and judgments must prevail. It's not surprising if this habit of needing to be always right sometimes spills into working relationships with other colleagues. This is an occupational hazard.

On the other hand, we should remember what teachers do. The whole point of their existence is to support, advise and extend other people. That is what they're happy doing. So, in approaching your mentor, you should bear these two characteristics in mind.

Cerian was frustrated with her progress. She felt that her mentor meetings lacked focus and progression. In fact, the conversations seemed to be only about behaviour management. Cerian felt that she wanted to be talking more about subject pedagogy, but they only ever talked about discipline.

This was quite perceptive of Cerian. It's actually a very common problem; the feedback after the lesson turns on whether the children behaved, how they settled, whether they stayed on task, which rewards-and-sanctions routines the trainee should have been applying, how she should behave differently to grow a more authoritative persona, and so on. This isn't surprising; these are pressing issues and, as is frequently said, the best planned lesson is pointless if the kids aren't listening. Trainees are of course preoccupied by these issues and are anxious to talk about them, but lesson feedbacks need to move from the immediate and obvious if the trainee is to move forward. Cerian felt this wasn't happening for her.

We talked about how Cerian should approach her mentor. To complain or to appear to criticise her mentoring may not be productive. On the other hand, to make a request for help would be a positive and professional approach. Cerian explained to her mentor that she felt that she needed help in extending her subject knowledge and wanted advice about how subject planning could underwrite a good classroom atmosphere. She asked if this topic could form the only agenda item for their next meeting (single-item agendas are a very good idea). Thus the positivity of the relationship was preserved while the content of the feedback moved on. There's nothing devious or manipulative about this – it's simply being professional. *If you have to raise a difficulty, don't criticise: ask for help.*

Lesson feedback is at the core of this relationship. Your mentor (and other teachers) will watch you teach and talk to you in some detail about what they've seen. Often these conversations drive the training. They should take place in a private place, and relatively soon after the lesson. The best feedbacks stem from observations which have been focused on specific developmental targets, though they are bound to cover other issues. What's the best use of these feedbacks?

We've mentioned being positive and being kind to yourself. Erin tells me that her mentor is always negative and this is depressing her. I watch her mentor giving feedback to her. The feedback is peppered with compliments and positive observations, along with some useful points for improvement. Later, privately, Erin says, 'You see? He hates me!'

As well as seeking positives in your own reflection, you must listen for the positives in what's being said to you. The habit of just not hearing compliments is very common, probably deriving from stress. You have to explicitly organise your own mental hygiene. Write down the good points. If necessary, at the end of the conversation, ask your mentor to summarise three good points as well as two development areas from the lesson. Close the conversation with this explicit balance. Take control.

How else should you make best use of feedback? One of the most important success indicators on a training course is the ability to listen, and one of the commonest barriers to progress is defensiveness. The people around you know more about the job than you do. Listen to them.

This isn't as obvious or as patronising as it sounds. Often, feedback conversations run like this:

MENTOR: Your starter was well planned, but you didn't really explain how it linked to the rest of the lesson. We need to think about transitions between activities.

TRAINEE: That was because we ran out of time and I really wanted to get on with the main activity because I knew they'd enjoy it ...

MENTOR: The lesson was well focused but there wasn't much variety of activity. It was pretty much all you talking to the whole class. We need to talk about how you could break that up.

TRAINEE: Well, they're a bright class, and I had such a lot to get through, I didn't have time for group work and all that ...

It's understandable and legitimate to want to argue your case, and of course you want to show that you have reasons for what you do. However, responses of this kind, as well as irritating your mentors, betray a fundamental misunderstanding of what feedback is for. In fact, *feedback* is not a good term: the word implies a looking back, while actually the whole point of such dialogues is to look *forward*. Your mentor isn't raising these points so much as a critique or review of the lesson but as an agenda for future development. Answering with these specific, backward justifications, though a wholly understandable and human tendency, is one that denies the necessity to discuss and develop issues within your teaching. Such responses are defensive, and no defence is required, because there's no attack. A good mantra for feedback is *another place, another time*. Try to think not of what you did or didn't do and why but of what might improve your teaching of another class in the future. It can be difficult to rest your agenda and take on someone else's, but often it's precisely then that you move forward the most.

It's important to be assertive but remember that assertiveness doesn't come from ignoring the answers to your questions; it might occasionally come from challenging those answers; but it most reliably comes when you ask the right questions in the first place.

We've covered some of the pressure points in your relationship with your school. In summary, it's worth taking an overview of your position within its structure. At university, you are the centre of the operation. As an undergraduate or, indeed, a trainee teacher, you are the focus of your tutors' considerations. In a placement school, this is simply not the case. The central factor at school is the children; teachers have many professional preoccupations and it has to be

said that trainees are not at the top of their list of concerns. That's not to say that your mentors aren't committed or conscientious or that they won't do their best for you; but structurally you are in a different position and this may be a considerable culture change for you. I mention it not to depress you but, on the contrary, to remind you that when your mentor forgets to say 'good morning', he's not ignoring you, he's just busy.

Working collaboratively

One of the advantages of being a trainee is that it provides many opportunities for working with other colleagues. Working collaboratively with fellow trainees, mentors and teachers, teaching assistants, parents and other adults provides much information and inspiration for your reflection and allows real penetration into the teacher's job. It's much more then 'team teaching'. *As in all training activities, you should drive the collaborative working by setting focuses for it.* Do you need to develop behaviour management (for example) or lesson planning? Which particular features of planning? Find a collaborative activity which will specifically support chosen aspects of your development.

Table 4.1 suggests some collaborations. They are only suggestions; you can devise your own models based on them. (In fact adapting or devising your own procedures is almost always a sign that training is going well.) Many terms used in this list have not yet been defined in this book; don't be alarmed by them; look in later chapters for fuller explanations.

Remember that you could be A or B in every case; there's no 'lead' collaborator; so swap roles often. Try also to vary your collaborator, covering a range of people from the list above. The table separates activities; in reality, these will often be shared , but one of the advantages of working collaboratively is the focus that comes from taking responsibility for specifics. This avoids the danger of collaborative work degenerating into several people staring at a blank piece of paper, constantly disagreeing and starting again!

Integration

Your course will consist of various elements, such as lectures and seminars in subject studies and professional studies, school placements, written assignments of various kinds, subject auditing,

Table 4.1 Collaborative working

Theme: Lesson planning

Focus	A	B
Parts of a lesson based on agreed learning objectives	Plans the starter and plenary	Plans the main activities
Using learning objectives	Decides on appropriate objectives	Plans the lesson
Group work	Decides on appropriate objectives	Devises appropriate group work
Questioning in lesson with agreed outline	Devises main activities	Focuses on a range of appropriate questioning
Health and safety on agreed lesson outline	Highlights health and safety issues in plan	Focuses on solutions to these issues
Differentiation in lesson with agreed learning objectives	Devises outline plan	Modifies plan for enhanced differentiation
Inclusion in lesson with agreed learning objectives	Devises outline plan	Modifies plan for enhanced inclusion
Focusing on pupils' reactions and experiences	Devises outline plan	Considers effectiveness of use of pupils' attitudes and experiences
Understanding transitions in lesson with agreed outline	Devises key activities	Focuses on key transitions between activities
Working on EAL on agreed lesson outline	Devises key activities	Modifies plan for enhanced EAL
Evaluation of lesson with agreed outline	Devises starter and main activities	Focuses on evaluation throughout and on plenary activity

Theme: Planning and teaching

Focus	A	B
Lesson planning	Plans lesson	Teaches lesson
Feedback	Teaches	Observes and gives feedback
Teaching a jointly-planned lesson	Teaches starter, plenary	Teaches main activities

continued...

Table 4.1 continued

Theme: Planning and teaching

Focus	A	B
	Acts as teacher	Acts as teaching assistant, e.g. for SEN or EAL
	Teaches half the class	Teaches half the class
	Teaches most of class	Teaches specific small group
	Teaches and supervises whole class	Takes smaller groups for guided group work
Teaching a sequence of lessons	Plans and teaches lesson 1	Plans and teaches lesson 2
	Plans lesson 1, teaches lesson 2	Teaches lesson 1, plans lesson 2

Theme: Medium- and short-term planning

Focus	A	B
Creating a short-term plan	Draws the plan objectives from the medium-term plan and creates short-term overview	Plans individual lessons to objectives; gathers resources
Resources	Creates overview of short- or medium-term plan	Lists necessary resources for plan and allocates resource creation tasks to A and B
Creating a medium-term plan	Draws learning objectives from long-term plan; discusses with B; divides short-term planning between A and B	Creates half of the short-term plans, as allocated, and evaluates scheme before and after teaching
Planning for good behaviour	Plans a lesson to agreed objectives	Evaluates lesson plan; looks for danger zones; looks for motivation and interest points; checks level and appropriateness; modifies plan for good behaviour

continued...

Table 4.1 continued

Theme: Medium- and short-term planning		
Focus	A	B
Teaching	Teaches	Observes with behaviour focus
On-task behaviour	Teaches	Observes and records on- and off-task behaviour

Theme: Assessment		
Focus	A	B
Assessment for learning	Marks work Sets work	Develops next lesson Discusses work with pupil
	Sets work	Sets up peer assessment criteria
	Takes an overview of single pupil's work	Sets a level or grade for single pupil's work

reading educational theory (see below) and, possibly, building evidence of your achievements. This poses significant organisational challenges. More fundamentally, it can lead to confusions and apparent inconsistencies in the demands made on you.

There's no doubt that trainees who struggle include those who can't find the connections between the different parts of the training. Frequently these trainees become bogged down by what they see as inconsistency or irrelevance. They will say, 'OK, so I don't write good assignments. So what? I'm good in the classroom ...' Or, 'I don't see what all this theory has to do with it. I get on really well with the kids ...' Or, 'Why does my university tutor keep banging on about learning objectives? None of the teachers use them and my school mentor says they're pointless ...' Spending long periods in school, they may forget about issues (such as inclusion, differentiation or evaluation) raised in their central training. The training becomes divided in their minds between the school-based 'reality' and the university-based 'theory'. This situation can last for weeks or months; it can seem at first to be a way of coping through prioritising but, inevitably, it ends badly.

Trainees who succeed are the ones who find the links. It's a good idea to start from the position that all aspects of your training are important. If you can't work out what the connections are, then ask somebody to explain them. As a matter of principle, whatever the type of training you've chosen, it isn't an apprenticeship. You aren't just watching and copying. Teaching is a profession, like medicine. Consider the occasional stories of people who pretend to be surgeons. They turn up at hospitals in white coats and assist in operations, though they have no qualifications. Sometimes this goes on for years; they even carry out basic surgery, until finally someone realises what's going on, and the bogus doctor is arrested. Do you want to be operated on by someone who has just watched and copied? He might look like a doctor, he might even be able to remove an appendix, but can he make a diagnosis? Can he do anything beyond what he's seen? Most important, what does he do when the operation goes wrong?

A profession has a body of knowledge attached to it. In teaching this will be found in school but also in educational theory, in evaluation and reflection. In particular, your training will become effective when your practice is based not simply on what you've seen and tried but on what you've read, criticised, discussed and evaluated. You can't possibly encounter every type of child, every problem and every opportunity just through practice. You have to draw on other people's experiences and expertise as well.

A good training course will go some way to making these connections for you. School mentors should support the fundamentals of the central training and not seek to undermine them. University teaching and assignments should be strongly linked to school practice. Professional and subject studies should reinforce each other, perhaps by looking at principles (such as differentiation) in professional sessions and then at subject applications of those principles in subject sessions. The more explicit these links are, the greater the sense of purpose and security in your training. However, you may well have to make many of these connections yourself.

Let's take the crucial example of *learning objectives*. A working understanding of these is so important to your training that they're mentioned in every chapter of this book, with particular detail in Chapter 5. But it's an area rife with confusion. There are various similar terms, for a start. There are *learning objectives*, but there are also *intended learning outcomes*. For some people these are different things, but sometimes the terms seem to be interchangeable. Then there are *assessment objectives* which sometimes are the same as learning objectives but sometimes aren't. And then there are differing definitions. For some people, *draw a map* is a learning objective. For others, it's an intended learning outcome; and for yet others it's neither of those – it's just an *activity*. So we have a group of terms variously used by various people.

This is dispiriting, but the problems can and must be solved. It's tempting just to walk away from all this – if the experts can't sort it out, how can you be expected to? And the disparity isn't just one of definition – it seems also to be one of attitude and practice. Your (university) tutor wants you to plan every lesson from learning objectives. Your (school) mentor says that's just a bit of theoretical nonsense and you should be planning activities. He teaches extremely well and doesn't ever think in terms of objectives. So the next temptation in your attempt to resolve all this is to go with one side or the other. You will stick with what your tutor says, though this will lead to tension and confusion in school. Or you will follow your mentor, though this will apparently mean ignoring crucial aspects of the training programme. Neither course seems very comfortable.

This kind of confusion is an inevitable part of a trainee's experience, even in the best organised training environment. As we said in Chapter 1, this needs to be seen as an aspect of the richness and diversity of teaching. You will find your own approaches and your own persona, and it won't be the same as anyone else's, but the journey towards this is a difficult one. Advice that is apparently contradictory simply reflects the massive creative variety that makes teaching exciting. This is true, but as you sit wondering where to start planning your next lesson, it's not much help.

As we've said many times, you have to take control. Assertiveness comes from asking the right questions. If learning objectives are so important, why is your mentor so disparaging of them?

Work collaboratively with your mentor on planning a lesson. Sit with him as he plans. Ask him to talk you through the planning decisions he makes. It may be years since he's had to articulate some of these thought processes. Ask him why he's chosen the lesson activities. Watch him teaching. Ask yourself what the children are actually learning. What journey does the lesson take them on? What are the connections between the various activities in the lesson? What does the teacher talk about in the transitions? Does his questioning check that they're getting the point? If so, what point are they meant to be getting? In other words, watch the planning and the learning *to see where the lesson objectives are.* They are there, though perhaps the mentor isn't explicitly aware of them.

Perhaps he's been teaching so well for so long that he knows from habit, experience and instinct that certain activities lead to certain learning. As a mentor, he needs to unpack that for you (because you don't yet have habit, experience or instinct) but, if he isn't doing that, then you can do it for yourself.

If the lessons are working, then the learning objectives (or whatever they're called – who cares?) must be there. The inconsistency is superficial – you've asked the right questions and found the links. Now you're moving forward in terms of your own understanding of how crucial principles are enacted in classrooms. Any good teacher is using learning objectives, even if he doesn't realise it. I know this from experience. For twenty years I thought that objectives were slavish and limiting and what mattered was spontaneity and creativity. It wasn't until I became a trainer of teachers that I began to see the centrality of them and to realise that they were and always had been embedded in my own practice. I had to stand back from my teaching in order to see it. Perhaps you can help your mentor to do that. In so doing, you will often find that apparent contradictions disappear. The learning objectives were there all the time.

It's helpful if mentors remember the differences between you and them. You have to plan your lessons elaborately on pro-formas (see Chapter 5) but you notice that nobody else in school seems to plan them much, if at all. This doesn't mean that planning lessons is an academic luxury for which there's no time in the real world. It may mean that experienced teachers don't need to think as formulaically as trainees or to write as much down. If teachers around you forget that your needs are different – *specifically, that your practice has to be more explicit than theirs, to help you grow into an understanding of it* – then you need at least to keep reminding yourself of this distinction. Perhaps you need to remind them as well.

This range and apparent inconsistency isn't confined to university/ school disagreements. You may find it in the advice offered by teachers you work with in the same school, in the same department. One teacher says, 'Don't talk over them. Never talk over them. They have to be quiet and listen to you. If they talk, you stop and wait for quiet before you go on.'

It's good advice. There's no point in talking if people aren't listening and you have to signal that things aren't as they should be if you want the children to be quiet – we will discuss this more in Chapter 6. You are teaching them basic courtesy and gently showing who's in charge. You accept the advice and put it into practice. It seems to be going well until Year 9 on Wednesday.

Year 9 talk. You talk; they carry on talking. You ask for quiet. They are quiet; you talk; they start talking; you stop. They carry on. You raise your voice. They shut up. You talk; they start talking; you stop. After four minutes of this, no start of any kind has been made on the work. In her feedback, your mentor explains that your tactic had in fact handed control over to the class. They were in charge. They knew that if they spoke, you stopped talking, and so no work came their way. So the good advice given by teacher A is now contradicted by teacher B. What are you to make of this?

What you make of it is that all advice is welcome, all strategies are worth considering, and contexts alter cases. None of this was bad advice but there is no advice that is always good. If there were, there would be one book about teaching; everybody would read it, and everybody would be brilliant. Unfortunately, there is no such book – not even this one. There are no absolutes. This is reassuring – it means there's room for experiment and individuality.

Make creative and critical use of advice. As we said with lesson observation and feedback, the process only has meaning when you evaluate it and relate it to context. What you have to do here isn't grumble that they all tell you different things, but rather try to understand the direction and purpose of advice and decide where it's appropriate to try it out. If it fails, you learn by working out what went wrong. Don't ignore it, but don't follow it literally or slavishly – make it your own. Teacher A's tactic works perfectly with Year 8. With Year 7 it needs modifying by the introduction of rewards points. With Year 9 it really doesn't work at all, and *you have to consider why this is so.* Perhaps they are less motivated anyway, perhaps you need to provide more accessible opening activities which require much less explanation from you, work they can settle to without needing to listen to you. Perhaps the work you're asking them to do isn't interesting; perhaps it's too difficult; perhaps it isn't sufficiently differentiated. There isn't one tactic for good lesson beginnings or for anything else, and advice that states that there is needs to be taken only with a pinch of salt.

You have to move beyond pragmatism

In early practice training, pragmatism is all you've got. Your targets are: get Year 8 marking done, get resources sorted for Year 7, get Year

9 to listen, get some rest. The pragmatic agenda is necessary because it's how you survive. It also seems to be how real teachers function – they don't sit around discussing Bruner (see the next section), they just get on with what they have to do. But you have to remember that they are different to you. They have watched pupils learn, develop and change over a period, they have seen results (in several senses of the word). They evaluate and modify all the time – it's an inevitable condition of the job. All of this affects their work. So their pragmatism is a rich and informed pragmatism. Yours isn't.

It's common to feel, after the initial flush of pragmatic adrenalin (which can last for weeks or months), that you're drifting. The pragmatic approach is no longer enough. Your targets need now to move beyond the immediate and urgent so that you rediscover a sense of purpose. It's at this point that you need to reconnect with the principles of your training. Such principles as objectives-based planning, theories of how children learn, differentiation, inclusion, assessment for learning and evaluation are discussed elsewhere in this book. Teachers apply all of this to their day-to-day functioning, but they probably do it implicitly and even unconsciously. You have to do it explicitly. It's time to go back to the central principles, perhaps to the university training, and to reconnect it with your school practice.

Ideally, your training should have mechanisms which force these connections, but you may need to make them yourself. Relate written assignments to school experiences if you can. Go back to those early lecture notes and try out some of the ideas in the classroom. A common phone call for me is:

DESPERATE TRAINEE: I've got to teach Romantic poetry next week and I've no idea where to start. Please help me.
TUTOR: What about the approaches we discussed in university last October?
DESPERATE TRAINEE: Blimey, I'd forgotten about them.

A week later, he phones me to say that it went brilliantly. After months in a school placement, he'd entirely separated the central training from his school work. This drift into pragmatism is a bad thing, because it leads to fragmentation, it's limiting and you can't rely on it. Once again, you have to take control. When confronted with a university task, ask yourself how it can be related to your school practice. When struggling at school, go back to the theory or to the university training; you may be surprised by the solutions it holds.

All that theory

Arguments in favour of 'theory' are made in the 'Integration' section above. Nothing that you do or see in a classroom doesn't concern one learning theory or another. Theory embodies the thinking of people who have spent lifetimes working out how best to help children learn and you can't seriously embark on a teaching career without it. However, there's a lot of it, it doesn't appear especially attractive or accessible, and you don't have much time to read it. So what are you supposed to do?

You need to think about theory as part of the solution, not as part of the problem. It has things to tell you which will help your teaching. One good thing about theory is that, because it's *learning* theory, not *teaching* theory, it focuses your attention where it should be. To start with, try to think on a personal level. You could begin with some preliminary thoughts about your own learning. You

could remember key learning experiences from your past (and these may well not involve formal teaching at all – there's more learning in the world than there is teaching) but a better way is to *try to learn something new*. As a trainee teacher, you are bound to have knowledge gaps to fill. These might be subject knowledge gaps; they might be gaps in other professional areas – such as information and communications technology (ICT). You might be uneasy with using computers (and teachers have to be comfortable with them – this isn't optional); or perhaps you can't use an interactive whiteboard. Start your own learning mini-project and monitor your learning.

In evaluating your own learning you will make some preliminary judgments about what makes learning happen, and what obstructs it. You will be considering the various outside resources available – books, libraries, television, friends, manuals, web sites, software, help files, DVDs – and you will be considering issues within yourself that either helped or hindered the learning. How do you make sense of an instruction manual? Do you prefer that to having a friend explain things? Why? Which activities give you most confidence? How do you get a sense of progress? How do you deal with frustration? How and when do you define a new skill as 'learnt'?

It would be even more effective if you could conduct your learning project alongside a friend who's doing the same thing. In comparing your evaluations you will define commonalities and differences, both of which will help you towards understanding how learning works for different people.

Such a process of learning and reflection should take you to a level of personal analysis. You should make some judgments about what suits you best. Do you like diagrams, tables, pictures, music, rhymes, repetition, stories? What part does language play in your learning? Are you translating the new ideas into your own words? What part does your existing experience play in your learning? How important are examples or models? Do you need to relate the new ideas to things you already know? You can't learn web site design, for example, unless you can work a computer.

Such analysis may give you some new teaching ideas but, more significantly, it will help you to create a makeshift and tentative theory about learning. Armed with these preliminary thoughts, you should now consider what other people have to say about it.

This isn't a theoretical text book. Other books, such as *Learning to Teach in the Secondary School*, offer detailed accounts of significant education theory; and, of course, you should deal with the primary texts themselves when incorporating theory into your training assignments. As you begin to look at theory, some of it will resonate with your own thoughts about learning. Theory is based on extensive research and links to scholarship in various disciplines – it isn't just common sense in fancy language. Nevertheless, it is in the end about people, and it's reassuring when it looks familiar.

Theories of *types and styles of learning* are currently widely in use in schools. If you ask a teacher about Bruner or Vygotsky he may struggle to remember the names, but staffrooms are full of work based on Gardner's *multiple intelligences*. We will consider this more fully in Chapter 8, but for now it's a helpful place to start thinking about how theory connects to practice.

This is a theory that can be grasped in basic form in a few minutes. It looks like common sense. Different people learn things in different ways. Therefore it's a good idea to offer a range of access routes to key pieces of learning. Explain things in different ways. Offer a range of activities. Vary your language.

There's no doubt that multiple intelligences is immensely popular or that it's generated excellent work in schools. It's easy to see why. It's an accessible theory that is simply translated into practice. It offers straightforward solutions to current issues. The UK government, for example, is strongly committed to the principle of *inclusion*, and this connects directly to teachers' preoccupations with *differentiation* (see Chapter 8) and both of these issues are addressed by multiple intelligences. School initiatives centred around it have led to school-based discussions on learning theory which (it has to be said) have not always been the common currency of staffrooms. At the very least they have made some teachers vary their teaching styles, and they have involved pupils in thinking about their own learning, which is certainly a very good thing.

There is some concern that multiple intelligences (or its little brother, VAK) has been overdone, or that it hasn't a firm and rigorous basis in scientific or psychological theory. It's true that some schools have bought into it in extremely systematic ways and there may be something dehumanising about every child in Year 7 having his own defined learning style. I haven't seen children wearing badges but it's only a matter of time. I was watching a lesson recently. A little boy was wandering around the class, pausing randomly to hit fellow-pupils with a copy of *David Copperfield*. The class teacher, who was sitting next to me, was beaming at him. 'He's a kinaesthetic learner', she explained to me, lovingly.

Nevertheless, multiple intelligences is a good starting point for your consideration of theory because it shows how principles of learning can easily affect classroom practice.

Vygotsky

Vygotsky's work – an aspect of *social constructivist theory* – concerns what he called the 'zone of proximal development'. This 'zone' stands between the pupil's current learning and the next level. Any teacher must be thinking about how the 'zone' is to be crossed – how the learner is to move on. A central answer for Vygotsky involves language, especially talk. Perhaps you found this in your own learning analysis; perhaps you make best sense of a new idea when you talk about it. You literally translate new ideas into your own language, using your own examples. For example, as you read this, you might be thinking of an instance of coming across a new idea and restating it so that you understood it. In remembering that example, you are actually applying the process to the ideas in this paragraph. When you say, 'Oh yes, that's like when I had to talk to Paul about the difference between a spreadsheet and a table, and he said, "Well, a spreadsheet is really a mathematical thing, and a table is a formatting thing", and I said, "Oh, you mean a table is more presentational, but spreadsheet does calculations and things" ...' you are actually translating this paragraph into your own language. When you spoke to Paul about spreadsheets, you were doing the same thing.

In practical terms, this aspect of Vygotsky places talk in a central position and this has direct implications for your lesson planning. Where is the talk, and how is it structured? At a very basic level, I never set a task for students without asking them to discuss the task in pairs, and then to raise queries about it. This routine adds about ninety seconds to your task setting but saves much time, misunderstanding and wasted energy. Try it, and eavesdrop. And think about when your lecturer tells your class to do something. Don't you immediately need to say to the person next to you, 'What does he mean? Does he mean like this ...? Is he talking about ...?' and so on. Let the children restate the task in conversation with each other. Let them re-explain key concepts, redefining them in their own terms. The power of simple pair-work is enormous, and in using it you are showing your understanding of social constructivism.

Bruner

Bruner offers specific thoughts about the conversations that might happen between pupil and teacher. The teacher offers *scaffolding* to prompt and support the learner through a curriculum which grows through stages of complexity as the learning matures. The teacher adjusts her talk with pupils by (for example) asking questions and making spontaneous interventions to point children in the right direction, and these exchanges diminish as the learning becomes more assured.

It's a helpful metaphor; the scaffolding is essential but temporary, allowing the building of the learning to get off to a safe and confident start. As you observe lessons, you should look out for it. It may be formal, and addressed to the whole class, especially in the early stages of a piece of learning. Some of my trainees think of scaffolding as bicycle stabilisers. For example, the teacher may offer a writing frame which provides a fairly prescriptive format for a history essay. Such a frame may be based on the topics and first sentences of a sequence of paragraphs. It means that everybody can get started and that most people's worries about how to structure the essay are reduced. They know what order to put the paragraphs in, how each paragraph should start, how they should talk about historical evidence, and where their conclusion should be. But the scaffolding may not end there. The teacher should also be running individual and group-based conversations which allow him to offer prompting questions and suggestions around the room; the scaffolding moves from whole-class, formally structured scaffolding to semi-spontaneous, individual support. Certainly a formal scaffold like a writing frame has limitations – it can restrict creativity and originality – and the teacher's individual conversations may need to compensate for this. At some point, the scaffold will be removed.

So you should consider where and how you need to scaffold. There are several recognised stages of scaffolding. The current UK Secondary Strategy – including the National Literacy Strategy – favours scaffolding; so there is a useful example of how an aspect of social constructivist learning theory has been taken up in curricular policies and enacted in schools.

Of course, it's just common sense that pupils need particular help in getting started. Beginnings are very important in teaching. Your lesson plans should begin to show your scaffolding methods. They might include writing frames, examples, sets of written instructions, prompt scripts, shared or guided writing, models and demonstrations. In one day (as you might know, from pupil shadowing) a pupil may be asked to write three *essays* (or assignments or sets of notes or reviews) and each one of the three, set by a different teacher in a different lesson, will have different requirements. A history essay in the morning looks and sounds fundamentally different to an English essay in the afternoon. Schools work very hard to reduce such confusions, but there will always be a range of definitions and variation of requirements. One thing that you can and must do is define what you mean, for example by 'essay'. That is as much a part of the learning as the subject matter of the essay itself. This defining process is often best delivered through scaffolding.

These aspects of social constructivism (so called because you build (construct) the learning by (social) interaction with other people) form the basis of most currently accepted learning theory. In referring to them in your writing, you should show how you have observed, used and evaluated their practical application. For example, you could compare lessons with strong pupil-talk with lessons without it; or you could try to teach with and without explicit scaffolding, and consider the different outcomes in pupil learning. Sustained, comparative and evaluative application like this is much more effective than occasional quotations. You can even challenge the theories – for example, you could examine the shortcomings of prescriptive scaffolding (such as the over-use of writing frames) and the questions it poses regarding pupil originality. Setting out to use the best advantages of scaffolding while devising techniques to allow for pupil variation would be a fascinating response to theory which both embraces and challenges it. This is far stronger than simply dragging in the odd line to (apparently) justify a decision in lesson planning. It's also quite sophisticated – you wouldn't expect to be doing this in the early stages of training.

Constructivism

It's worth considering one or two other areas of theory in terms of what they can offer you as a teacher. General constructivism emphasises that learners take on new information by relating it to their own existing ideas. This is a significant factor in lesson planning. I was recently watching a geography teacher introducing the idea that towns vary in function and character – for example, they are ports, or industrial towns, or holiday resorts. The lesson was in fact taking place in a town which had all three of those functions, so all the pupils were already familiar with this diversity, though they had probably never thought explicitly about it. Every day they saw the containers and cranes of the port, the lorries and factories, the beach, the tourists and the chip shops. Children are walking round stuffed with information and brilliant teachers respect this and capitalise on it. This teacher tried; he showed them photographs of parts of their own town, but he insisted on defining the concepts for them. He asked them how they knew that their town was a port, and the answer (which he quickly supplied) was that it exported and imported goods. He pointed at a photograph of the cranes to underline this.

This is a try at using pupil experience, but it could go so much further. The teacher is preoccupied with the definition of port and jumps to it almost immediately. Similarly, he told them that their town was industrial because it made things. But in providing these definitions so early he is preventing the pupils from constructing their own understanding based on their own perception and experience. How do you know that the area you're looking at is an industrial area? Do you think, 'Hmmm. They're making a lot of things here; this must be an industrial area'? No: in fact, you're more likely to think, 'What a lot of lorries and factories. Not many houses. Definitely industrial.' You know a port because you spot the cranes on the skyline, not because you're aware of the economic activity. As a non-geographer, I am already equipped to make preliminary judgments about towns and their functions. As a geographer, you have to consider how non-geographers like me think.

My point is that the pupils already knew that towns had different functions. They knew that people visited their town for their holidays, and that they didn't hang around the factories when they came. All the teacher needed to do was to add prompt questions – What are those cranes *for*? What are they *doing* in those factories? – to build the lesson concepts onto the pupils' prior knowledge. There may seem little difference between defining a port as a place that exports and imports things and defining a port as a place with ships and cranes. Indeed, the second definition may seem naive and incomplete, but it is the second definition that begins to build on pupils' understanding. The new definition has a chance of bonding and staying because the brain is able to find a place for it.

Assimilating, storing and accessing information

Other learning theories have grown up around the idea of how we might assimilate, store and access information. Some of them clearly relate to our knowledge of how computers do similar things. An area I find particularly apposite concerns how we encourage *concept differentiation*. This is a progressive aspect of maturation. A new baby doesn't distinguish between itself and its mother; an adolescent certainly does and it's possible to define learning as a growing understanding of the differences between things. This highlights the absolute centrality of *comparison* in good teaching.

Look at the stick man in the first picture. What can you tell me about him? Almost nothing. But from the second picture (overleaf) you can tell me that he's probably a *little* stick man. The comparison immediately provides information. Brilliant teachers find the right comparisons. To understand that towns have different functions, you could of course consider one town. You could consider the function of Liverpool. But it's a lot easier to compare it with Birmingham, which has no big river, no cranes, but a lot of factories. *Comparing two things is always more than twice as good as looking at one.* You're looking at Blake's poem *London*. What's the mood of this poem? What does Blake think of London? How much easier to look at Blake's poem alongside Wordsworth's *Westminster Bridge*, which is also about London. Immediately it's clear that Blake is miserable and Wordsworth is happy. Even if, as teacher, I don't much care about Wordsworth or Birmingham I'm going to put them on the table to sharpen up the defining process.

Connected with this is the notion that we process new ideas via *examples*. You might look through this book, or this theory section in particular, and mark every time I've used an example. I would suggest that often those are the moments where it all starts to make sense. Learning theory is by nature rather abstract; so are new ideas for children, and one way of mitigating this is to provide concrete examples which relate new concepts to existing knowledge. *A good example is worth a thousand definitions.*

Let's put these thoughts together into a piece of literacy teaching (because we are all teachers of literacy). You want your pupils to complete a piece of *formal writing* and you notice that they aren't too sure about this. They perhaps even ask, 'What do you mean by it?' So you have to take time to introduce the idea of formal writing.

The worst kind of teaching would proceed from a definition. A definition could be found and written on the board. It would say something along the lines of:

> writing which is appropriate to formal situations or which assumes a formal function and audience, avoiding colloquialisms, and adopting standard grammar forms.

Of course, this is ridiculous; no pupil who needed to know what formal language was would find it out this way; but how often are you depending on definitions of one kind or another? *Definitions are things you move* towards, *not starting points.* So what's a better approach?

First of all, we are going to use a constructivist approach which relates to pupils' prior knowledge. In this case, pupils already know about language appropriateness. They already know that they use different language when talking to the head teacher, to their friends and to their mums. The beginning of the understanding about formality and informality is already there; you just need to spend some time on it. For example (you see, there I go again), you could make a list on the whiteboard and arrange in order of formality – head teacher at the top, sibling, friend, girlfriend ... – and then you could talk about the differences. What would you say to your girlfriend that you wouldn't say to the head teacher? It's not just about the subject matter, it's about the language. Pupils know all about these games. They're experts.

At this point you can if necessary define formality; it now has a meaning for them in terms of their own lives. You could then show them the beginnings of two pieces of writing, one formal and one informal (perhaps just two sentences, written on the board) and they could talk about them in pairs, compare them, and draw conclusions about formal writing.

You may say that, as a science teacher, you haven't got time for all this; but that's a separate argument (except to say, teaching three things well has a meaning, and teaching eight things badly doesn't). This approach is progressive, constructive, and makes effective use of examples and comparisons.

In fact all the theory in this section has a meaning to me as a teacher and I have to make a confession here. I read all of it after twenty years of successful school teaching. I was already using all of the techniques included here – pair work, interventions, scaffolding, talk, pupil experience, comparisons and examples – because they all seemed to me to make for successful learning. I was delighted to find, when I became a teacher trainer, that I was working within respected theoretical frameworks. But it took me years to make all of these discoveries, and I wish somebody had pointed me at the theories sooner – it would have saved a lot of work.

Danger signs

Below is a list of signs of trouble which mentors, trainees and I have drawn up over the years. It's an empirical list of behaviours that are often harbingers of difficulty. Keep an eye open for them, but be careful. Very good trainees will exhibit some of these symptoms from time to time. Remember also that trainees move at different speeds. Your peers may seem to be forging ahead while you're still trying to pick up the basics. Don't worry about this – your time will come. It isn't a race, and in fact it's quite common for the slower starters to prove the stronger teachers in the end.

Failure to prepare and plan to deadlines so that plans can be seen by mentors

As well as the professional issue of meeting deadlines, this concerns the need to discuss and evaluate plans before teaching. You don't want your feedback from mentors to consist largely of what was wrong with the lesson, and one way to prevent this is to modify your planning in line with their suggestions before the teaching happens. You can't do this if they only see the lesson plan on the morning of the lesson.

Tendency to be unavailable for informal discussions

Are you hiding away at lunchtime? If so, you perhaps need to consider why. Be seen.

Tendency to resist advice or react defensively to it

This is covered extensively earlier in this chapter. Listen to your mentors and be sure that they see you acting on their advice.

Effort disproportionate to results: excessive time spent on planning, or very little

In the earlier stages you may well spend hours planning a ten-minute starter. This shouldn't alarm you, but as your training progresses, this proportionality should adjust itself. Keep a check on this. At some point, you will hit parity – one hour's planning for one hour's teaching; you should note this and have a bottle of wine. In the final stages of training, this should have swung almost full-circle and you should be spending ten or fifteen minutes planning a one-hour lesson. The rate of change varies, but you should discuss your planning if you aren't making progress.

Continued dependence on peers or mentors for lesson ideas

This is another 'journey' (see Chapter 2) and, again, it's impossible to predict. In the early stages you should be seeking advice wherever you can find it; teachers always need to exchange ideas; you don't have to apologise for this. But in the second half of your training you should note how often you need to ask for lesson ideas, or how dependent you are on the internet or text and course books. Mentors will be concerned if you aren't three-quarters independent in the last quarter of your training.

Collecting evidence

In the UK, all teacher training is designed to provide at least Qualified Teacher Status (QTS) and for this to be recognised you have to meet the standards for QTS (see Chapter 1). It's important that you understand from the outset how your training course intends to provide evidence that the standards have been met. Even if you aren't training within a jurisdiction which is based on prescribed standards, the building of a portfolio of evidence is a likely requirement, and a good thing, for example in gaining employment after your training.

The creation of the standards is an odd project. Writing everything that teachers need to be able to do in a series of statements may seem impossible, insulting, inaccurate or irritating. As with so many of the potentially annoying aspects of your training, the trick is to make them work for you. They do provide a focus, they can suggest new ideas, they can keep your mentor on track, and they do provide a common language for talking about teaching. Anyway, you're stuck with them, and with providing evidence that you've met them by the end of your course.

There are various approaches to this, but they fall largely into two types. One is the holistic approach. In this case, the training ensures coverage of the standards in various components and will ask you to provide sample evidence of your experiences. This may well include the requirement to write reflectively about your achievements (see below), but it will not require a statement of evidence against every single standard. A second, more atomistic approach is one that requires you indicate how and when every individual standard has been met. This is likely to include a grid of all of the standards which will be signed and dated. Some training courses combine aspects of both of these approaches. Be sure you know what's required of you, because you probably need to start gathering evidence quite early on.

To support you in gathering standards evidence you need to be sure that the standards are being used in as many areas of your training as possible. Evaluate training seminars in terms of the standards. Evaluate your own lessons and the lessons you observe with reference to them, and ask your mentors to use them in their written feedback. Indicate on your lesson plans and schemes of work which standards they are demonstrating. Use them to define your target-setting regime. The more often they appear, the easier it will be for you to select relevant evidence later on.

To do this, you will need to interpret the standards as you go along. Incidentally, they are reviewed from time to time and it's possible that any examples used here are of standards which have been altered since the publication of this book. However, the principles of their purpose and use remain the same. They may seem extremely formal, quasi-legalistic in their expression, but usually they can be interpreted in terms of practical common sense and evidenced from your normal work at school or university. For example, a standard such as this:

> (Teachers) have high expectations of all pupils; respect their social, cultural, linguistic, religious and ethnic backgrounds; and are committed to raising their educational achievement.

appears formidable at first glance; it's a mixture of compression and generalisation and doesn't make easy reading. To evidence such a statement you need to unpack it and specify areas within it. *Where will you find evidence of this saintly behaviour?*

The most common source of evidence is the written observations of your teaching provided by your mentor. If you have asked him to refer to standards, this will make it easier; but, even if he isn't doing this, you need to go to his written feedbacks. He might at different times say that:

- you are polite to pupils;
- you listen carefully to their contributions in class;
- you set challenging work;
- you have well targeted learning objectives;
- you have clear behaviour routines, for example at lesson beginnings;
- you pause the lesson to remind them of good behaviour patterns;
- you use praise and encouragement effectively;

and any of these comments may be taken as evidence for the first part of this standard – that you have high expectations. The next part of the standard – concerning the pupils' varying backgrounds – may appear much more challenging; but if you look again, you may well find that your mentor already considers that:

- you set a variety of tasks within the lesson;
- you involve pupils' opinions and experiences in the discussion;
- you use a variety of teaching styles;
- you use pair work effectively;
- you show respect for varying opinions in the discussion;
- you model and demonstrated effectively;
- you check learning and understanding as you go along;
- you build an atmosphere of openness and tolerance in the classroom;

and so on. So the standards can usually be resolved into good classroom practice.

Lesson observations aren't the only source of standards evidence and you may be asked to provide evidence which is more varied and perhaps more substantial. Other forms of evidence could include your observations of other teachers, your lesson plans and work schemes, copies of children's work, reflective writing of your own (see below), video or audio records of your work, resources, notes of meetings and training events, annotated policy documents and annotated theory or research readings.

At best this is evidence of progress as well as of simple achievement. Strong *composite evidence* could indicate change and development in your practice. An early feedback from your mentor indicates that you aren't responding positively to children's contributions. They answer your questions, but you tend to ignore their opinions, having a very limited sense of the 'right' answer and rewarding only that. This is discouraging for pupils whose opinions are being snubbed. You read up about this, and you discuss it in detail with your mentor. You then design some lessons which are based on pupil opinion and you script quite carefully how you're going to handle and validate a range of opinions in the room. The lessons are taught and the feedback records improvement in this area. Such developments might well go on for some months. In such a case, a valid set of evidence would contain:

- the initial critical observation;
- notes of the meeting where it was discussed;
- annotated readings, for example of Vygotsky;
- consequent lesson plans;
- copies of children's work;
- mentor feedback commenting on progress;
- reflective writing about this development.

This is a rich sequence of progressive evidence which attaches to a number of the standards, including the one we happened to quote at the beginning of this section. Remember of course that even a single piece of evidence is likely to cover several standards.

Reflective writing

Teaching is an individual business, so learning to teach isn't just the linear acquisition of a set of pre-ordained skills. The central driver of your training is your ability to reflect personally on your experiences, to analyse them and to make plans and targets as a result. This reflection is necessary to your development as a professional and should continue through your teaching career.

This happens in a range of contexts, including discussions with your mentor, but your course is very likely to require it to happen in writing as well. After all, written reflection requires personal focus and concentration as well as providing concrete evidence that reflection is happening. However, trainees quite often find it difficult to get started with reflective writing.

One of the main issues here is that of confidence. Trainees think that they can't do reflective writing. They suspect that it has a particular set of formal requirements which they haven't met before. But this isn't true; there are some conventions which allow reflective writing to happen, but they are based on common sense, and are fairly flexible. You may in the past have been confronted with quite specific formal requirements ('Never write in the first person!') for academic writing but the expectations around reflective writing are much more diverse and relaxed. It is, after all, essentially personal. *If you can think about what's happening to you, and try to understand why and what to do about it, you can do reflective writing.*

Let's first of all consider the *content* of reflective writing. Its purpose, as we've said, is to examine experiences and draw developmental conclusions. The experiences in question are varied. You may, for example, reflect on lessons that you've observed, or on lessons that you've taught. You may reflect on conversations, reading, your own planning, other people's planning, meetings or training events. Just about everything that happens to you provides some food for thought.

Naturally, this richness makes it necessary to make some choices. One way of doing this is to consider your own specific targets over periods of your training. You might want to select events which have impacted on a chosen focus. You found it hard to motivate disaffected children, but you have made progress in this area. Or you have made great improvements in your subject knowledge. So now you have to make a list of the experiences which contributed to this development. Alternatively, perhaps there have been some memorable, critical moments in your training – moments when things started to work, when corners were turned. These could be key lessons, key conversations, key readings, key lectures – moments when the penny dropped, when the scales seemed to fall from your eyes. These critical events may be many or few in your experience of training. You could base your reflective writing around them.

Reflective writing then is personal and may even be anecdotal up to a point, but this doesn't mean that it's not rigorous. In particular, it needs to be analytical. The line between description and analysis troubles some trainees, but it's not really difficult. *Writing becomes analytical when it asks the question why?* It's also precisely at this point that it becomes useful to you.

Consider this extract:

I wanted to begin with a recap of the previous lesson using pair discussion. There were some discussion prompts and questions on the desks to get them started. However they didn't settle very well, and one boy was so disruptive that I had to report him to the class teacher. They didn't really answer the questions and in the end I had to quieten the class and remind them what had happened in the previous lesson as well as telling them that I wasn't very pleased with their attitude. They did finally settle down to the main task, which was reading and understanding a source text, and then the lesson went quite well.

This is a genuine and sincere (and early) attempt at reflective writing and it clearly shows a trainee trying to think about her experiences. It's not a bad starting point, but it is descriptive rather than analytical. You might try counting the number of times this piece skates over the question *why?* I think it does so eight or nine times. Try a similar count on your own writing if your tutors are telling you that you need to be more analytical. Why did she want a recap? Why did she want it to be in pairs? Why were there written discussion prompts? Why did the pupils not settle? You may not need to answer every question, but dealing with some or most of them will produce a far more mature and considered piece:

> I think that a recap is always essential. Children have had many school and non-school experiences since last lesson and need to refocus to establish continuity. On this occasion I wanted to use pair discussion to involve all of them in doing more than just listening to me and to give them a chance to support each other. I decided to place written prompts on the desks so that they could get started immediately, without the need to listen to me at all, and so that they knew exactly what to focus on. However, the recap didn't really succeed, and, on reflection, I think that the class needed a brief spoken comment from me to create a more definite beginning to the lesson. Listening to them later, it also became clear to me that the prompts I'd given them were too challenging and they had been unable to work with them without help.

It's obvious how much stronger the second piece is; real reflection is now beginning. You'll notice that there is analysis of both expected and unexpected events. The trainee can offer ready explanations of why she did certain things – after all, she must have had her reasons. But she also has to reflect on the pupils' unexpected behaviour. This is less immediate, but she comes up with some possible explanations (and she omits the purely anecdotal incident of the naughty boy).

Of course, she could strengthen the reflection even further by considering other sources of analysis. Perhaps she discussed the poor reaction to her starter with her mentor; or perhaps she did some reading which helped her to understand what went wrong. So, in a third stage, she could involve (for example) some theory.

> On this occasion I wanted to use pair discussion to involve all of them in doing more than just listening to me and to give them a chance to support each other. I think that this is consistent with Gardner's thoughts about 'multiple intelligences', in that I'm offering a teaching style which is not my usual one and which might suit those who favour interpersonal intelligence. I also think that this pair work reflects social constructivist ideas, where the pupils are sharing and building their own understanding.

Here, theory is used to support trainee decisions; you should also use your reading to help you to analyse unexpected outcomes:

> They didn't really answer the questions and in the end I had to quieten the class and remind them what had happened in the previous lesson as well as telling them that I wasn't very pleased with their attitude. Jon Davison (in Capel, Leask and Turner) comments on the central importance of 'the establishment of ground rules to prevent misbehaviour'. My mentor commented afterwards that, by beginning the lesson without teacher talk, I missed an opportunity to gently remind them of my expectations. Davison also mentions rewards and punishments; on this occasion, I could have used the school sanctions system, which might have restored good behaviour at an earlier stage.

So, to recap, we have three levels of reflective writing:

1   Your diary (straightforward description of what happened)

2   Your diary
    PLUS personal analytical commentary (asking why?)

3   Your diary
     PLUS personal analytical commentary
     PLUS the use of reading and theory (extra help with your analysis).

Wherever you start, you will need at least to move beyond the first level.

Reflective writing in the UK may also focus on the QTS Standards (see above). A useful formula here is to use your writing to explain your evidence. A standard requires that you:

> set challenging teaching and learning objectives ...

and you provide a piece of evidence for this. This could be composite evidence – say, a lesson plan, a mentor observation and a piece of pupil self-assessment from the same work. Your reflective writing explicitly connects the evidence to the standard, for example:

> The learning objectives on this plan were intended to be differentiated, which is why there is a range of pupil activities. There were choices for pupils, but I guided the choices, because I particularly wanted some of the more able pupils to be challenged. In their cases, there are choices which took them from concrete to more abstract work and required them to synthesise different sources of information before offering their own judgments about it. My mentor comments in his written feedback that 'you managed the choices well, and the very able boys in particular were challenged by the additional objectives'. In fact David writes in his self-assessment log, 'I found it difficult to put the different ideas together and we had to talk a lot about that, but I think I learned some new skills from it'. This evidence therefore indicates that I can meet the required standard of *setting challenging teaching and learning objectives*.

Having discussed what you might write about, let's briefly consider the *style and structure* of reflective writing. Perhaps it worries people because it's an odd hybrid, seeming to be both formal and personal. In fact, this means that there are fewer rules about it than most types of writing, and a range of possible approaches. The tone of it is fairly straightforward and conversational. You are bound to use the first person; you are writing an analytical diary. It's fine to abbreviate (as long as you use the apostrophe correctly!). You should talk to the reader as if he is an interested and intelligent non-expert. Try your writing out on a close, patient friend. Even if he's not a teacher, he should understand the points you're making, just as (I hope) he would understand this paragraph. Nobody expects you to be overly formal. The rigour of the writing comes not from a solemn tone or fancy vocabulary, but from analytical thoughtfulness.

Another way of improving your reflective writing is to become more aware of *structure*. One problem is that the writing can become simply a chronological account with analysis thrown in – what might be called a *running commentary*, rather like a football commentary – goal, analysis of goal, foul, analysis of foul, missed goal, analysis of missed goal, goal, analysis of goal. This can provide reasonable reflective writing at level 2 of the three levels listed above, but it can tend to weaken the focus of the analysis. For example, it might be useful to analyse all of the goals together, to compare them and to see if there's a pattern, or to compare the two goals with the missed goal to analyse the strengths and weaknesses of the forward line. At the planning stage (any decent writing requires planning) you should be considering how you might structure your writing to enable more sustained discussion.

This is often just a question of thinking of sections. These might become different sets of paragraphs; they might even appear as sub-headings. For example, the extract given above is the account of a single lesson but it covers at least two major areas. It covers issues of *planning* the lesson and also issues of *teaching* ('delivering') the lesson, and it makes no real attempt to separate them. This works up to a point, but it does tend to mean that the chronological account is driven by events and that bits of analysis which don't have much to do with each other are stuck next to each other. You could consider dividing the account in two. First of all explain and analyse all of the *planning* decisions. Then, take the reflection into the classroom and comment on what happened in the *teaching*. This kind of structure may mean that your analysis can jump among bits of the lesson, linking and comparing them. For example, you will find that your thoughts about a planning issue – for example, the nature of the tasks that you set – can pick up points from the beginning, middle and end of the lesson and string them together, allowing you to draw more sustained and thought-out conclusions and to see patterns in your own task-setting practice. As well as creating better reflective writing, this is bound to be much more helpful to your development than disjointed, chronological thinking.

This simple separation of *planning* and *teaching* is a quick way to add depth and structure to an account of a lesson. There are other structures, of course. You could organise your reflection into thematic sections – for example, sections on *questioning*, on *task setting*, on *motivating pupils* – and any such structure will lift the writing away from the limitations of chronological running commentary. In creating any such structures you will be using your writing to support your own development and to sustain the reflective process, which is the single most important process in your training.

Chapter 5

Planning

We said in Chapter 2 that planning is the most important thing a teacher does. Bad planning will more or less guarantee poor learning and (incidentally) bad behaviour, and good planning will improve both. In the early stages, planning will take up far too much of your time, but you have to accept this and work through the process. It will get better.

Of course it may seem possible (and alluring) to do no planning at all. The internet offers a wealth of lesson plans and various government strategies seem happy to tell us what and how to teach. You can also use textbooks which present attractive courses with plans for you and resources for pupils, and indeed your school may well have medium-term plans in place which they want you to draw on. To an exhausted trainee, downloading or photocopying prepared materials may seem like a lifeline and, from time to time, it's a reasonable tactic. Life's hard enough without reinventing everything.

However, you should consider the limitations of overusing other people's materials. For one thing, it's actually quite difficult to do; trainees who are required by their schools to teach ready-made lessons often run into trouble and realise that they can't make good sense of them. What had seemed like a godsend becomes a frustration. Beyond that, simply working through a textbook or website sequence reduces your role – you have become an administrator, not a teacher. And of course the point of training is to understand how teaching and learning works. If you simply run other people's systems you will gain little insight into the processes behind them; this is karaoke, not teaching. Most important of all, you need to design lessons which will suit the individuals and classes that you teach. Of course, this can (and must) involve other people's ideas, but each lesson plan should contain somewhere a unique dialogue between you and your pupils.

Planning backwards

This is easy to say, but as you stare at a blank sheet of paper, with sixteen lessons to plan and no ideas for lesson one, it's not much help. Stop thinking about lesson one! At all levels (and there are about four levels), *planning starts at the end and works backwards.* The *Secondary Strategy*, for example, proposes a hierarchy of planning (long-, medium- and short-term planning) which implies the need for planning backwards. You start from knowing what the long-term learning objectives are, and these are interpreted in ever-increasing detail down the hierarchy. So your blank sheet of paper doesn't exist. You already know what you're going to achieve at the other end, and this will enable you to get started.

As a trainee, you are unlikely to be involved with long-term planning, but the medium-term plan will lie behind most of your work. It covers the learning objectives for a period of weeks, perhaps half a term; some schools will call this a scheme of work, and it will cover one or two central themes or topics. As a beginning trainee you may be asked to plan individual lessons (or lesson parts) within the medium-term plan, so it will provide you with background ideas. If you aren't given one, ask for it, and use it to take away the panic of the blank sheet. As a more advanced trainee, you might well be asked to design medium-term plans of your own. The medium-term plan lists the learning objectives week-by-week; each separate week then becomes a short-term plan, which will break the week's objectives down into individual lessons. So these are the four levels: long term (a year or more); medium term (a half-term or a term); short term (a week); and lesson plan.

It's good that the various subject frameworks and strategies put forward this straightforward planning system. Important concepts lie behind it. One is that good teaching depends on clear learning objectives. Another is that brilliant teaching needs not just good lessons but good sequences of lessons. The lessons must hang together, and it's the objectives that link them. This is all very encouraging, but you might be wondering how such prescriptive planning systems can deliver the kind of individuality and creativity we were talking about earlier.

In fact, creativity is more important now than ever. The prescriptive systems need to be individualised if the teacher is not to be reduced to a supervisor or administrator of other people's activities. It isn't hard to do, and it happens at two levels. First, teachers are involved in setting up the medium-term plans. These are not prescribed by outsiders. If the school has them, they will have been written to suit its pupils. Furthermore, they can (and should) be revised constantly. As an advanced trainee, you should be modifying or even originating medium-term plans for your department, and these will reflect your own enthusiasms and your sense of your pupils. But don't panic; you won't be able to do this at the beginning, and even experienced teachers often do it in pairs.

Second, you will see that your subject framework doesn't offer lesson plans. The planning of individual lessons remains your province. However careful the overall planning, there is room for your personality within the lesson plan itself. Trainees become brilliant when they learn to craft individual lessons, and we will look at this in this chapter and the next.

Keep it simple

You won't be able to create perfect lessons from the outset, but there are some routines that will help you along. Of course, you should be watching other teachers and, ideally, planning with them. Look at how simple or complicated the successful lessons are. A common problem for trainees is over-complex lesson plans which defeat both them and the pupils. Often, this comes from a desire to include everything in the lesson. Keep it simple. Objectives will help you to do this.

Objectives – *Catch and Carry*

Learning objectives are your planning friends. They help you to keep a clear focus; they tell you what to do, what not to do, and what order to do it in. Trainees who prosper are those who understand this at an early stage. Once you have a clear sense of what the children will *know, understand* or *be able to do* by the end of the lesson, you will find it easier to construct meaningful activities.

Think of this as 0–60

The children come into the room; in sixty minutes they will leave, and they must leave carrying something they didn't come in with. I think of this (still, after all these years) as something physical, a small but valuable object that I've given them to take away. I imagine them walking out with it, in their hands or their pockets. Actually, that's why I prefer the term *objective* to its more fashionable parallel, *intended learning outcome*.

If, at the beginning of your planning, you can't define that object, your plan will have no shape or system and the pupils won't make sense of it. Picture the objective. For one thing, it's *singular*. One objective is enough, though two or three are acceptable. I once saw an advertising expert demonstrate the significance of *limiting the message*. He threw eight sponge balls at a member of the audience, who (naturally) caught none of them. He then threw a single one at somebody else, who caught it with ease. If you're listing more than two or three objectives for your lesson, think of all those balls bouncing out of sight under the seats. Your objective must be *small* enough to catch and carry.

It's also a *valuable* object. This means that it's been carefully chosen as essential to the learning and to have a meaning for the people you're giving it to.

Focus makes learning happen. If you're teaching people to play the guitar, then your *aim* is that they learn to play the guitar. This may well be your long-term objective. But as they walk in for their first lesson, your immediate objectives have to work in terms of one hour. In one hour they can (perhaps) get a sense of how to hold a guitar; understand what a chord is; and learn to finger the chord of E major. That's not bad going for an hour, and it gives you three clear objectives around knowledge, skills and understanding. You can now focus on your teaching approaches. At the end of the hour, they can hold up their guitars while making the E chord, you can immediately evaluate your teaching; and they can leave happy that they achieved what you intended, rather than bewildered by the size of the task ahead of them.

In fact, it's interesting to note that what looks like one learning objective is often two or three. I so often see teachers jumping over essential bits of learning, confusing everyone because they haven't considered the stages the pupils need to go through. There's no point in learning the chord of E if you don't actually know what a chord is. There's no point in looking at what the isobars tell you about Siberia if you don't know what isobars are. You can't understand the ambiguity of a particular Shakespeare scene if you don't know what ambiguity is. You need to unpick crucial bits of learning and assemble them in the right order. Sometimes these are separate objectives.

Small is beautiful

Where do objectives come from? Often they begin life in subject frameworks, interpreted into medium-term plans; but you can and must rewrite them. The more local and specific the objective, the better. If the plan objective concerns grammar, you need to say which particular bits of grammar. If the plan objective concerns drawing maps, you should say which specific maps, or which specific features of maps matter for your class today. If you are considering the technical aspects of poetry, your own objective must say precisely which technical aspects in which particular poem. Objectives sometimes seem to daunt trainees, and this may be because of the grandiose and generalised language in which they get written. Such language isn't meaningless, but it doesn't tell you what to do on a Thursday afternoon. Take the objective and rewrite it in your own language for your lesson with your class. Bring it down to size, so that it can be useful to you. The smaller it gets, the better. This specificity is essential to your planning and the children's learning. Some teachers will say that they haven't time to limit the learning in this way and they will plough on with teaching everything that comes up, every feature of the map, every aspect of the poem, every historical fact and argument. It can feel quite satisfying; the children have lots of notes, they appear to learn lots of things; time well spent. But consider 0–60; exactly what are they carrying out with them? Are they going to drop it? *And think also of 0–24.* What will they remember tomorrow? Are you going to teach three things well, so that they can carry them away and, if their mums ask them what they learned today, remember them with clarity? Or are you going to teach twelve things of which they'll forget eight and confuse the rest?

Let's look in more detail at a final example of the value of local and specific learning objectives, and how to create them. This particular example is based on the *English* Framework, but the process is generic, so do stick with it, even if it's not your subject.

You are going to read the famous *I have a dream* speech of Martin Luther King. You are studying this as part of a medium-term plan which considers persuasive texts; so next week you might be looking at television advertisements. What links King to televison adverts is that they both seek to influence their audience to take action of some kind, and you are looking at certain ways in which the various writers do this. King's speech is in fact extremely structured and uses key features to make an impact, just as advertisements do.

The Framework objective, in the medium-term plan, requires pupils to:

> analyse the overall structure of a text to identify how key ideas are developed, e.g. through the organisation of the content and the patterns of language used.

This is typical of the language of objectives. No wonder people are wary of them. Like a number of head teachers I've worked with, they are both powerful and vague at the same time. As a statement of learning, this grand objective is far from irrelevant; it explains why you're reading King; but it offers few thoughts on what you might actually do with him in your classroom. *You need to supplement the generalised objective with a specific one of your own.* You need to decide to annotate this big objective, deciding *which* content and patterns of the speech can be appreciated by your Year-8 pupils, and which might best be left alone. *What you leave out is as important as what you leave in.* Be selective. Like a sculptor, you chip away until a shape emerges.

Here is part of the speech:

Five score years ago, a great American, in whose symbolic shadow we stand signed the Emancipation Proclamation. This momentous decree came as a great beacon light of hope to millions of Negro slaves who had been seared in the flames of withering injustice. It came as a joyous daybreak to end the long night of captivity. But one hundred years later, we must face the tragic fact that the Negro is still not free.

One hundred years later, the life of the Negro is still sadly crippled by the manacles of segregation and the chains of discrimination. One hundred years later, the Negro lives on a lonely island of poverty in the midst of a vast ocean of material prosperity. One hundred years later, the Negro is still languishing in the corners of American society and finds himself an exile in his own land.

So we have come here today to dramatize an appalling condition. In a sense we have come to our nation's capital to cash a check. When the architects of our republic wrote the magnificent words of the Constitution and the Declaration of Independence, they were signing a promissory note to which every American was to fall heir ...

Whatever your subject (and, by the way, I've seen this speech in English, history, PHSE and citizenship lessons) this is a remarkable piece of text. In preparing to teach it, you might decide that your pupils will respond to key features such as the repetition (of various phrases, not just the keynote line), the sustained metaphors (for example, the metaphor of the cheque) and the strong, figurative language. You might on the other hand decide that the powerful use of antithesis (opposites) will be too challenging for them at this stage and you are going to leave this out. *You are making decisions about how to focus the objectives.* You are not including every possible feature; you are creating defined and focused learning which they can *catch and carry away.*

So your lesson will begin with two main objectives; the given Framework objective above and your own *specific, local rendering of it,* which might be:

> Pupils will understand and appreciate King's use of repetition and metaphor, for example, the metaphor of the cheque.

This second objective sounds less grand than the first, but it grows from it, and it provides a basis for planning your activities. It allows you to focus absolutely on a couple of issues. You can work on repetition, not just in the speech, but in life in general. Teachers use it; comedians use it; adverts use it; fairy stories use it. You can build activities which go beyond the material itself into other contexts, but always holding tight to the basic objective of repetition. The lesson now is growing around proper learning concepts, fully delivered and roundly exemplified, rather than slogging through and making notes on every possible thing as it comes along, explaining everything briefly and nothing properly.

Try it. Try teaching everything and then asking the next day (0–24) what they remember. Then try the same test with a simple lesson based on one, two or three linked objectives, properly explored. There's a chance that, when tomorrow comes, they'll be able to bring it back.

Some myths about objectives

It's very difficult to think them up

The objective is what the children learn. If this isn't the basis of your teaching, what is? But objectives don't have to sound grand, general and academic, and the most useful ones don't.

They spoil spontaneity

They provide focus and continuity but any lesson can undergo radical changes in the delivery. The ones that do are sometimes the best ones.

You can teach perfectly well without them

This can never be true – how can you teach without planning for pupil learning? – but it's interesting to consider why it gets said. Experienced teachers say it; I thought it myself for many years. The fact is that good teaching often gets done by teachers who are using objectives implicitly. They devise activities which produce good learning and already have a sense of what pupils are getting out of them. Their good teaching will become even better when they recognise that they are already using objectives and begin to plan explicitly around them.

You have to write them on the board at the start of every lesson

You should always know and plan from your objectives, but your lesson plan might not require the pupils to know them from the start. Lessons should often have an air of exploration; pupils are working towards the objectives, not recovering from an initial definition of them. In fact the mechanistic reputation of objectives may stem from the rigid lesson shape which demands their initial publication on the board and final evaluation where pupils dutifully report at the end of the lesson that they have, indeed, learned what they should have. Sometimes, if the lesson is a story, the objectives are the hidden treasure.

You don't need them with sixth-formers

Of course, post-16 teaching is different. The pupils are volunteers; they love the subject; they love learning; you don't need to plan systematically; all you need is a gas fire, some marshmallows to toast and a schooner of medium-dry sherry to sip as they read their assignments aloud in the darkening afternoon.

You may have noticed that this is a fantasy, but it's not an uncommon one. Post-16 teaching requires all of the planning, structure and focus of the rest of your work. It certainly requires local and specific learning objectives, and here as elsewhere they are a support to collaborative and focused teaching.

Planning is imaginative!

As you sit in your bedroom planning, you have to consider the third of the three planning elements. The first two – you and the material to be taught – are present and accounted for, but the third – the pupils – are only in your head. In fact all plans (wedding plans, career plans, holiday plans) are essentially acts of imagination. You are projecting what should and what might happen; you are guessing at the possible reactions to and repercussions of your decisions. You are anticipating good and bad outcomes. Lesson plans are no different, and they only become alive and effective when you recognise their fundamentally imaginative nature.

This may sound whimsical but it has systematic, concrete implications for the efficiency of your teaching. It means first and foremost that you are creating events and experiences for pupils, not broadcasting information to them, and at every planning stage you should be imagining their possible reactions, associations and confusions. So your lesson plans need to distinguish between teacher and pupil activity. You need to consider their access routes to the learning, not just the content of it.

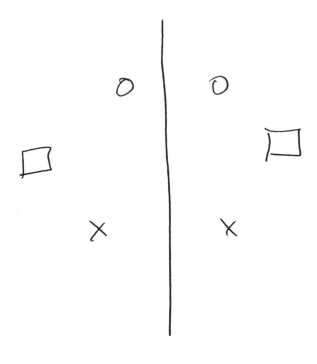

When training teachers, I always describe a particular Year-8 maths lesson which I saw years ago. It seemed (and still seems to me now) to be an object lesson in efficient, focused, elegant and objective-based teaching. The teacher entered the classroom and drew a vertical line down the middle of the whiteboard. He then drew a small cross to one side of the line. The children watched him as he paused; then he drew another identical cross opposite the first, on the other side of the line. After another pause, he drew another cross, somewhere above the original cross, and offered the board marker to the class. A few hands went up. A volunteer took the marker and drew the fourth cross, exactly opposite the third one. And so the lesson went on for some minutes, the children increasingly active. Not a word was spoken.

As well as being a maths lesson, this was also a lesson in literacy, and you should consider how often this is the case. At its simplest level, this can mean that a serious and early objective in your lesson may involve definitions – isosceles, attrition, compound, meander … You can't just dash off a quick definition and move on. This lesson was about symmetry, of course. It worked almost perfectly for a number of reasons. It had a single, clear and focused objective; it was highly interactive; it generated the need for a piece of learning and then met that need.

Let's consider that last point. The teacher could have come in and said, 'Today we're going to talk about symmetry'. (He writes the word on the board.) 'OK. Symmetry. What's symmetry? Does anyone know? No? Well …' And he proceeds to define and illustrate the word.

You've sat in that lesson dozens of times. I've taught it dozens of times. 'Today we're going to talk about metaphors. What's a metaphor …?' When you start considering the third element in the planning chain – the pupils – you start to see what an imperfect approach this is. 'The questions are irritating. I don't know what a metaphor is, no. If I did, you wouldn't need to be teaching it to me, would you? So why are you asking me? Don't you know? Don't you know what I know? Let's get on with it. Just tell me about the flaming metaphors.'

If you begin your lesson with the word, the concept, the key learning, you can only travel backwards. The lesson becomes a retrospective definition. Instead, plan your lesson to move forward towards the key learning moments. After six or eight minutes drawing crosses and then circles in varying positions and colours, the maths teacher started a discussion about the children's decisions. They explained to him, using words like *opposite, mirror, same place*. They reached a point where, in order to continue the conversation, they needed an appropriate word. The teacher, having created the concept, having explored it through activity, having generated the need for the word, finally supplied it. The pupils, rather than being bored, mildly interested, passive, were actively grateful. They were relieved, because they needed the word, and now they had it. When they went home that night, they would be able to tell anyone who asked them what symmetry was. We learn when there's a need to learn. We don't learn just by being told. We don't learn words from dictionaries.

Let's recap the features of this lesson. It is based on a single learning objective. It is interactive. It moves towards defining the key learning, not backwards from an initial definition. It creates a need for a piece of learning and then supplies the need. It has an element of game. It is structured and focused. It is self-evaluating. For these reasons it will pass the 0–60 and the 0–24 tests.

Is it difficult to create such a lesson? The point about it is its simplicity. Once he had the objective (symmetry) clearly in his head, the teacher could easily devise the activity. You should pause now and consider how you can apply the process. Look at a learning topic, and take a single objective from it. Then create an interactive activity which will move the class towards an understanding of that objective. Personally, I created a *simile* lesson; every child drew and labelled a simile on the board, based on a comical face (*eyes like fried eggs, spots like baked beans*) and then we defined, explored and enjoyed the notion of similes. Try it with your own subject, and remember simplicity – one objective, one activity, one clear piece of understanding to take away.

Chapter 6

Managing learning, managing classrooms

The trendy Hollywood teacher enters the classroom for the first time. The disaffected adolescents sneer at him and chew their gum but he is somehow different; he sits for a moment on the edge of the desk, he looks at them with patient humour, he has perhaps a small tattoo. He writes 'FREEDOM' in huge capitals on the board and, intrigued despite themselves, the drug dealers, muggers and amateur prostitutes who make up his first-ever class begin to offer thoughts on 'FREEDOM' as it relates to their inner-city lives. Soon, they will give up drug-dealing, mugging and amateur prostitution and form a close-harmony choir which will come second in a prestigious inter-state competition.

This character is as dangerous as he (or she) is charismatic. His agenda is about as wrong as it could be, but his influence is pervasive. He contributes to the miasma of apprehension and misapprehension that surrounds the whole anxious question of making good, working relationships with children. It is an issue that concerns trainee teachers more than any other.

Of course, your personality is significant here, and you need to think explicitly about your personal strengths and weaknesses; but teaching is a complex and subtle business, not a simple matter of energy, performance and attractiveness. Indeed, a classroom persona built mainly around such qualities is almost certain to fail because it excludes pupils, except as awe-struck audiences. It is certainly true that some teachers seem to have a natural sense of working in a classroom, and some look as though they will never be able to do it; but the majority of us can achieve success with hard work, and *this work lies in preparation more than in performance.*

You should never feel alone in a classroom. Schools have elaborate behaviour policies which only have a chance of working when teachers abandon the maverick-genius approach and work together.

Such systems can work surprisingly well. However, they are, for the most part, extrinsic systems, at some distance from teaching and learning. Brilliant teachers use them, but they also recognise that *intrinsic methods, methods that plan good behaviour and good relationships into the classroom work itself, are the best.*

Brilliant class management comes through the work. It recognises that, in the end, high-energy performance is unsustainable and counter-productive, punishments are something of a bluff, and the best rewards lie within the work, not in the deployment of a discrete set of 'management skills'. You want children to work and, if they don't, you have to consider their reasons for not working. They aren't many, or complicated. Children don't work either because they can't, or because they don't want to. Good planning (rather than charismatic delivery) makes work accessible, purposeful and enjoyable.

Get the level right

At its most obvious, this concerns the level of academic challenge in the work you're offering. One of the most common planning errors for new teachers is pitching work too high, and this is an area where you should seek advice.

But there's more to it than this. Brilliant teachers differentiate as a matter of habit (see Chapter 8) and differentiated teaching provides a range of access routes to learning. Embedded differentiation isn't about giving out three worksheets (clever, average and not-clever-at-all) but about allowing for choices and different learning styles in your approaches to tasks, instructions and explanations. The machine doesn't start until the penny drops, and the penny drops at different times for different people. It's a simple matter to develop the habit of explaining crucial learning or key instructions in three or four different ways. This needs to be planned in to your lesson.

The shape of the lesson: transitions and the lesson story

Children are motivated when they see the point (and it's usually a good idea to tell them what the point is, explicitly). You create a sense of purpose and direction by crafting shapely lessons around clear and local objectives. A lesson needs a throughline, a clear story which links the activities to each other and to the learning outcomes. You may need to be quite explicit about these links. Arguably, these links – often manifest as the transition points in the lesson – are the most significant learning moments, moments when the learning becomes explicit. *Good teachers plan activities but brilliant teachers pay close planning attention to the connections between them.*

There are various useful metaphors for lesson planning, such as the lesson as a journey and the plan as the route map, and these all suggest that the lesson is best thought of as a complex event made up of connected parts. The *lesson story* is another helpful planning metaphor. You should be able to say, at least to yourself, and probably to your pupils: 'We need to learn the following thing. First of all, we will do activity A. Having done that, we will be able to take a new piece of understanding from it, look at it, and try it in a different way in activity B.' *In the moment between the activities, crucial things happen.* The past learning is evaluated and made explicit, and then transferred to the next activity, where it will be extended, modified and developed. If you can't see this link between the two activities, you must modify your planning. If the pupils can't see it, they need to have it pointed out explicitly. But many teachers will simply close the first activity and begin the second. Have you seen that? 'Right! Well done! Put that away now, and have a look at this ...'

Here is a transcript I took from an English teacher. Her learning objective is that the pupils will understand what similes are and why they might be used. She has conducted an opening activity in which pupils have jointly drawn a face on the board and labelled it with similes. She has finished that starter and is now moving on to the main activity, which is to read a poem ('Timothy Winters') and explore its similes.

TEACHER (looking with the class at the images on the whiteboard): Well, that's quite a character, isn't it? Quite a fascinating character, we should give him a name, should we? What should we call him? And he's got, what's he got? Spots like ten-penny pieces, apparently. Says Laura. (Laughter.) And what's this, hair like grass. Which are, as we are saying, this way of saying it's like something, it gives you a picture, we're saying, it makes you laugh. Ears like toadstools, apparently. (Laughter.) We're saying they're called similes, because one thing is similar to the other, when we say it's like something, OK, we're calling that expression a simile. Ears like toadstools is a simile. And the spelling. Say simile, but spell siMILE. SimILE, like MILE. It makes it what, more ... (Pupil: Funny.) Yes, more funny. And perhaps more vivid. A picture in the writing.
And now we're going to have a look at another character, and you'll see he has some similes too. Look for his ears. Not toadstools. Also his teeth. He's called Timothy. (Distributes poem.)

In transcript this may appear laboured, even patronising, but the teacher has recognised that this transition moment is a key moment where the learning becomes explicit, where the objective rises to the surface for focused discussion, and where the next activity is deliberately connected to the last one. Children can see what is being carried across. The throughline, based on the objective, is revealed.

If activities are the bricks of the lesson, transitions are the mortar; and the wall falls down without the mortar.

The lesson beginning: the tumbleweed experience

There's nothing worse, nothing harder to recover from, than a weak beginning. You walk in, you ask your killer question, and the class just looks at you. You ask it again; a note of pleading enters your voice. The silence prospers; tumbleweed is about to blow listlessly across the room. I've died this death many times and the sense of apathy, of non-co-operation, is almost irresistible. Twenty minutes into the lesson you'll have enough momentum to get you out of a hole, but the first three minutes are vital, and you must *plan certain success into your lesson opening.*

It's easy to do: consider this checklist for your first three minutes

Start once, not two or three times. If you have to wait a minute, wait, and start cleanly.

Deal straight away with the whole group, not with individuals who want to talk to you.

They should all be required to work within three minutes. Work here doesn't necessarily mean write, but it means more than listening to you. Mark this moment on your lesson plan – *when does everyone (not just volunteers) have to work?* I have watched lesson after lesson where no one who doesn't want to is required to actually do anything (other than appear to be listening to the teacher) for twenty minutes or more. Of course, this is a serious learning issue, but it is also a management issue. Children with nothing to do will eventually misbehave. This can happen right in the middle of what appears to be a highly interactive starter if the only contributors are actually volunteers.

Work from your powerbase – centre front. If you leave it, expect behaviour to change (see 'Stirring the tea', below).

Plan the foothills. Here's another metaphor – if the lesson is a mountain, the opening is the foothills. Everyone must step onto the foothills, and everyone can, because they are seductively gentle and almost flat. You are coaxing an animal out of a cage. For example, begin concrete, not abstract. An opening question like, 'Why do we dream?' is likely to bewilder the class, but, 'What did you dream about last night?' is likely to provoke some answers. Start with concrete, anecdotal questions which go the pupils' own experiences. 'What was the last argument in your house about?' will get you started; 'Why do families argue?' may only induce the tumbleweed response. (Could you answer that question out of the blue? *Are you testing your opening questions on a willing friend or lover?*)

It's good to start with speaking and listening (and you should always try to avoid the temptation to use writing as a management weapon). But don't just ask a question and expect an answer. Allow a minute or two (literally – time it with your watch) of silent jotting first. Now everyone can speak, because they have written something down; you aren't left dependent on volunteers, and no-one can opt out if asked, because you can say, 'Just tell us what you've written down ...'.

Task setting: always QDO

A management blackspot is the time immediately after task-setting when, instead of standing at the centre-front and settling the whole class, the teacher finds herself dealing with a forest of individual enquiries. Children need a considerable amount of conceptual and practical information from you before they can begin something. In one day I recorded the following questions asked immediately after task-setting. Each is a perfectly reasonable question, and each is quite sufficient to prevent a pupil from getting started.

Is it in the back of our books?
Do you mean, a real person, or a made-up person?
How long does it need to be?
Is it based on the book or is it a new story?

Does it have to rhyme?
How long have we got for this?
Is it a sketch or a proper map?
How many pieces of evidence?
Is it set out like a playscript?
How do you set out a playscript?
Should I finish this other work first?
Is this for coursework?
Can we work in pairs?
Which page is that on?
Is it a happy or a sad ending?
Is it a formal letter?
Where do you put the address?

and so on. There are dozens more of these questions, and a good teacher tries to head them off with clear and full task setting, but it's impossible to anticipate them all. A brilliant teacher uses a routine such as QDO to solve problems with the whole class.

QDO stands for Questions, Deadline and Outcome

Pupils beginning a task should be able to ask about things they don't understand, know how long they've got, and know what's going to happen at the far end. This is embarrassingly obvious but parts of it are frequently omitted. Its regular use can have unexpectedly dramatic results in settling children to work.

Q: Questions

Q reminds you to ask if children understand the task, if they have any questions. Of course, children will frequently assert that they do understand, that they don't have any questions; and when you tell them to start, they will put their hands up and start asking. This just seems to be a trade-union rule for pupils – never own up to not understanding. So there are better ways of handling Q; for example, why not have pupils always discuss a new task in pairs, for thirty seconds, and decide if they have any problems? (Remember social constructivism?) Then they can raise their hands and ask. This is now a part of the task setting; no one has begun, everyone is listening, problems are being raised and solved for everybody. And then you can say to the class, 'Is there now anything that will stop you working when I stop talking?'

D: Deadline

D reminds you that pupils need to know how long they've got. This allows them to plan the work, obviously; it also provides them with an immediate sense of what you're looking for in terms of depth and detail. And of course deadlines are highly motivating. I am working hard now on this manuscript because my deadline is looming. So use your watch a lot in the lesson; deadlines generate creative energy, and they aren't restricting. You don't have to keep to them, after all.

O: Outcome

O is the part of QDO that is often left out. You check that children have no further questions, you tell them how long they've got; you should also tell them where the work is going. Outcome here doesn't mean learning outcome or objective; it means what will happen next. The outcome from a piece of planning might be a GCSE coursework assignment; the outcome from silent writing might be a class reading; the outcome from group discussion might be a feedback to the whole class. Teachers will almost always plan the outcome, but it's surprising how rarely children are informed about it at the outset. Starting off to discuss global warming may engage you. Starting off to discuss global warming knowing that you've got to reach a conclusion in twenty minutes is more engaging. Starting off to discuss global warming knowing that in twenty minutes you're going to have to discuss your conclusions with the whole class is even more motivating.

Talking to the class: using questions

Teachers rightly love questions. If I write 'How high is the Eiffel Tower?' you cannot help, momentarily, picturing it and thinking about an answer. Questions are difficult to resist. All teachers know that there are different sorts of questions – open, closed, convergent, divergent, factual, rhetorical, opinion-based, and so on; and using a range is a good thing. Children like the security of right answers just as much as they like the freedom of exploration and opinion.

What matters most is that *they understand what sort of question is being asked.* This involves the teacher in being open and straightforward about it. You ask a good question, but do you also say, 'There's no right answer to this question'? More to the point, do you sometimes say, 'This question *does* have a right answer'? Children don't mind, but they like to know. The least motivating process, but one I see frequently, is where the teacher asks closed questions as if they were open ones. She has asked for an opinion about something, but in fact *although she has asked for opinions, she really has one clear answer in mind.* As she takes answers from volunteers, she grazes the class until the right answer is offered. I have heard myself doing this so many times. To those pupils who aren't offering the right answer, I say, 'Ye-es ...' in a sort of rising diphthong, which anyone can tell actually means, 'Yes, but ...' or, in fact, 'No!' The children know by now that *they are not being asked for their opinions at all; they are being asked to guess the teacher's opinion.* When someone finally works out what that is, she gets an excited 'Yes!' that is fundamentally different to the earlier responses.

I have sat in many lessons watching this process, and I watch the reactions of pupils who have offered a perfectly good answer to the question. They have been asked for a relevant opinion and have volunteered one, only to be snubbed. Their expressions at these moments are revealing. The mood is one of subliminal irritation. If you don't value my opinion, don't pretend that you do. I'll think twice before I volunteer again.

Valuing and validating pupil responses

In fact, this whole area of listening to pupils is seriously important in building good classroom atmosphere. Consider the child who volunteers any kind of contribution. He is making a genuine and quite possibly a difficult commitment to you. There may be all kinds of peer pressure against putting his hand up. *You absolutely must reward this commitment.*

All teachers listen to pupils but the validating of pupil contributions needs to be explicit. Contributions to discussion are validated when their *content* is addressed. Often, the contribution is rewarded with praise, and this is helpful; the teacher says 'Good!' or 'Well done!' and moves on to the next answer. It's better then nothing, but a string of 'goods' punctuating a class discussion doesn't motivate at a

high level. What motivates is the teacher actually taking the time (a few seconds, probably, no more) to discuss what the pupil has said. When this happens – the teacher asks a question back to the pupil, clarifying and developing a point in the pupil's argument – not only is the learning being progressed, but the balance of relationship in the room is moving towards genuine conversation. 'Good!' is merely assessive; the teacher remains entirely in charge of knowledge and opinion, and so shouldn't be surprised if pupils seem reluctant to join in.

The use of the whiteboard as a repository of pupil ideas – a list of one-word reminders of what pupils have said – is a simple but highly motivating tool. The pupils' ideas are published; they remain powerful for a few minutes, rather than disappearing into thin air; there is a symbolism about their words appearing in the teacher's work space.

In all of these matters of running a classroom, what we are seeing is that good learning and good behaviour go together. In the end, if pupils aren't motivated by the work, they won't be motivated by anything. With especially difficult classes, this can be a long, slow process, requiring frequent re-working and compromise to bring your agenda closer to that of the pupils. It won't happen on the first day, even if you do wear an earring and odd socks.

Don't YAVA

We have said that all pupils need to be required to work, though this work may not be writing; it may, for example, be answering teacher's questions. I have often watched teachers YAVA for twenty minutes at a time, sometimes much longer; but YAVA requires nothing of non-volunteers. YAVA stands for *You Ask, Volunteers Answer*; hands go up, keen volunteers speak; the lesson can feel very lively; the teacher will often think that things went rather well. For a couple of minutes, this is an active thing to do; but it has a very limited life. If you're not volunteering, you know that no one is going to bother you. The keen participants at the front can do the work; all you've got to do is keep quiet and avoid the teacher's eye. Don't you remember doing that at school? I spent two years in chemistry staring at the grain on the desk while my fresh-faced chemistry mates rattled on with Mr Webster about molecules and compounds. Everybody was happy, including me.

This is a major learning issue and, as so often, it's also a management issue. One person opting out is a problem; in the YAVA classroom, typically one third of the pupils are participating. A majority doing nothing is a management timebomb.

So don't YAVA, even though you will see experienced teachers doing it all the time. Of course you must ask questions; of course you must reward volunteers by taking their answers and engaging with them; but consider the fundamental change in the mood of the room when you ask just one non-volunteer to answer. This isn't only a change for the one person you ask; it's a change for all the non-combatants in the room, who suddenly realise that they may be next, so they'd better start thinking and listening. Don't abandon your volunteers; but mix them with non-volunteers always when talking to the whole class.

Managing speaking and listening

Whatever your subject, you have a commitment to speaking and listening. Not only is it part of the Literacy Strategy, it's an essential tool for learning. It keeps children interested and involved. A teacher asked me recently why his Year 8 behaved so badly. We looked at his medium-term planning; no speaking and listening for five weeks. Children will talk; your best hope is to make the talk legitimate rather than subversive. So speaking and listening are your management allies. If you're inclined to the opposite view – that 'oral' work is likely to cause bad behaviour, and so best avoided with difficult classes – you're in danger of initiating a vicious circle. Nailing them down to silent writing may be a short-term fix but is simply storing up negative pressure in the medium term. I am often surprised by the limited range and quantity of talk in secondary classrooms. All subjects without exception need pair and group discussion, prediction, the expression of opinion, the sharing of concepts, the collaborative defining of new ideas. Think of speaking and listening as an arena – you could call it the *oral arena*. This is a place where new ideas can be checked, modified, trialled. It's extremely efficient to try things out here; ideas can be swapped and tested before they become crystallised into writing, which is much less flexible. Misconceptions can be caught and dealt with; ideas can be worked and extended.

There is no magic in the management of speaking and listening. It requires what all good teaching requires – careful planning, clear objectives, thoughtful structures, clear focus. As usual, behaviour is managed by the lesson plan.

Group discussion

Let's consider, for example, the management of group discussion. What are the management danger points? Children may not talk; some may dominate to the detriment of others in the group; they may talk about *Eastenders*; they may make too much noise; you may not be able to properly monitor or control the discussion. Setting aside the point that any good teacher takes risks from time to time, we can easily deal with these danger points by good planning.

Are you thinking about the formation of the group?

Four people is enough. Larger groups split or isolate individuals. Varying grouping is essential – friendship groups, mixed-gender groups, extravert/introvert mixes, random groups where you just meet somebody new to work with.

Are you helping with the internal working of the group?

Groups are so often given a topic and left to it. Here as ever you have to plan from the pupils' viewpoint. Will they be able simply to get on with it? Do you need to advise them how to proceed? Do they need to define their group roles, such as group leader, group note-maker, group arguer?

This last is a brilliant addition to group work. One member is appointed devil's advocate (though you might not use the phrase). His job is to listen to the arguments and counter them. This is fun but also creates a whole new dynamic in the discussions. You can create other generic roles as well – such as a group pacifier, a group problem-solver. It is worth taking time over the definition of these roles. For example, the group note-maker is more than just a dogsbody; it is her job to pause the discussion from time to time to recap and agree on the positions reached so far. The leader does more than simply keeping it going; for example, she must ensure that everybody speaks and is heard. Brilliant teachers spend time on these roles, preferably by creating role cards for all members of the group which define their responsibilities. Even members with no additional job have a role card which defines the whole business of offering views, offering evidence, listening to counter arguments, considering how to respond, moving towards compromise, and so on.

It may take you an hour to make a set of group-discussion role cards like this but you can use them over and over again and your pupils will become used to them and need them less and less.

Table 6.1 Discussion group roles

Leader	Ensure that everyone gets a turn. Ensure that everyone listens. Ensure that the discussion brief is covered. Watch the time.
Note-maker	Record the discussion. Pause the discussion from time to time and summarise it with the group, checking your understanding. Contribute to feedback.
Arguer	Listen to and challenge arguments and opinions. Ask others to justify their arguments. Offer counter-arguments, especially if the discussion is quiet.
Pacifier	Help leader and members to reconcile opposing views. Offer compromises. Discuss changes of view among members.
Member	Offer views and evidence for them. Listen to other views, possibly making notes. Modify your views if appropriate.
Feedback organiser	Work with leader, note-maker and all group members to organise feedback. Check feedback requirements. Keep appropriate notes. Remind leader and group of timing so that feedback can be addressed.

Are they preparing for the discussion?

They can prepare by making relevant notes which they bring to the discussion so they all have a flying start. Think about useful structures for this. A simple continuum – a line with *totally in favour of fox-hunting* at one end and *totally against fox-hunting* at the other, with a mid-point ready marked – will allow pupils to focus on where they stand. They put their personal marks on the line and write a few sentences explaining their decision; they arrive at the group discussion with this information already in place.

Are you structuring the discussion?

Pupils need clear structure. You need to break down the discussion into timed components such as ten minutes for opening comments, time for main discussion, and so on. But you also need to structure the content. The discussion may focus on a prompt sheet. The prompt sheet might be:

* a series of questions to answer;
* a series of statements to place in order of preference;
* a series of statements to sort into given columns;
* a series of continua (see above) for group agreement and completion;
* a series of statements (or a single statement) with which to agree or disagree;

and so on.

Do you QDO?

They need to know how long they've got, and they need frequent reminders. They need warning as they approach the end. In particular, they need advance warning of the nature of any feedback. Preparing the feedback to the whole class is a task in itself and they need help with doing this, including a time allocation for it. They can't have a lively discussion and then just cobble together a feedback at the last minute. They need help with its content; they need to think about purpose and audience; they need to practise it.

Are you monitoring the groups?

You will develop a sense of when groups are flagging and need your subtle and brief intervention. It's easy to tell whether a group has strayed off the point and often all you need to do is to go and stand near it. You need to combine your accessibility to the groups with your visibility to the whole class. Often, teachers set pupils off on activities and then plunge into the body of the room, kneeling at tables (which is a good thing) while the behaviour in the room drops as the noise levels rise. This can go on for twenty minutes and things get steadily worse because the teacher has effectively, almost literally, disappeared. Children need periodic sight of you to remember where they are and what the background structures are. Don't circle from group to group – for one thing, this makes your path predictable. Visit a group, then return to the centre-front and stay there; you don't have to speak, or do teacher-glaring; just be visible; then visit another group.

Of course, pupils will digress; they will talk about football and boyfriends, you have to accept this, just as you have to accept that their minds will wander when they're sitting in silence. Of course, when they're talking, at least you know what they're talking about!

Stirring the tea

You are the spoon in the teacup. If you want to stir the class up, you must move around. At that danger moment of starting up group or pair discussions, when you're wondering if they might just sit there self-consciously not saying anything (a tumbleweed moment) you need to get away from the centre front, start moving around. The noise will start. But when you need them to quieten down, stop stirring; stand still. I've seen so many teachers stirring the class up by walking around, kneeling, disappearing, while periodically nagging them to be quiet. You can't expect both; you can't stir the tea and expect it to remain stationary.

Listening

The groups have finished their discussions and prepared their feedbacks. Now each group will speak. In management terms, this is another blackspot. Children aren't especially good at listening to each other. Telling them to listen because it's polite to listen has limited power; children spend a lot of time doing things that aren't polite. Expecting them to listen out of genuine interest is optimistic. For one thing, listening to six feedbacks about the armistice is tedious, even if they're good. And it gets worse as the same points are repeated. Groups waiting their turn are likely to be more preoccupied with whispered preparation than with listening. Groups who have already performed are demob-happy. So how do we manage the listening?

For one thing, we vary the nature of feedbacks. We don't always have them; the value of the work is in the discussion process, not the feedback product. Or we only take feedbacks from some of the groups. Or we move randomly around the room. Or we have different feedback methods – my favourite is the envoy, where the single feedback-giver from each group moves around the groups, reporting to each one, discussing the issues, and then moving on. But really the point is not to have a favourite.

And second, we focus on the listeners. In any classroom where a child (or, indeed, a teacher) is talking and twenty-five children are listening, *the teacher's attention needs to be focused not on the speaker – he has something to do – but on the listeners.* Give them a reason for listening. Tell them they must make particular notes, or answer or ask particular questions about what they're listening to. They can be asked to guess something about the presentation, or to evaluate it. If we expect children to listen because they're interested, or because it's polite, we are likely to be disappointed.

Motivating pupils: joint ownership

You don't want to break a thing if it belongs to you. Children behave better if they have genuine involvement. Opinions, for example, are very motivating; children who frankly don't care why Jane Eyre behaves as she does will nevertheless have quite clear views as to how she *should* behave, and how they would behave in her situation. It's a scientific fact that adolescents are made up of equal parts of hormones and opinions, and almost every lesson in every subject can invite the sharing of the latter. Where is this in your lesson planning? It should be a regular feature, because it vigorously connects pupils to learning.

Particularly useful is the use of prediction. Ask pupils to predict the outcome of a story, an experiment, a historical negotiation. This can be individual work, pair work (better, for sharing) or group role play. Once a prediction is made, pupils have an interest in finding out what really happened, and comparing it to their own suggestions.

Quietness is golden

When children or adults are asked what they value in a teacher they rarely comment on subject knowledge. Instead, they talk about values – enthusiasm, approachability, fairness, organization. One important value is credibility. They have to believe you. Setting punishments you won't carry out is a sure way of losing credibility. Writing an ever-growing list of detention-names on the board is a credibility trap – are you really going to keep the whole class in? And asking for silence and not meaning it or not getting it is a way of handing control over to the pupils.

Silence is an absolute. Don't use the word as a synonym for quietness. Silence means nobody speaks, at all, for any reason. You may need pupils to be silent, and you can achieve this, so long as you take some trouble over it. You need to:

- explain what silence is, literally;
- *tell them why it matters, with regard to the particular nature of the work* (in terms perhaps of concentration, or privacy, or originality of thought);
- tell them for how long it's going to last – and this must be a short time, perhaps three minutes. Anyone can be silent for three minutes, but no one can seriously set out to be silent for an unspecified time – could you?
- ensure they're all prepared before the silence begins;
- watch them and use low-key control if necessary to maintain the silence.

You shouldn't ask for silence if there isn't a work-related reason for it; if you do require it, you must take some trouble over it. Like most management issues, it has to do with the content of what you're doing, and requires explicit but low-key handling in a collaborative atmosphere. Of course, it's naive to simply assert that appropriate work, well planned, will eradicate uncooperative behaviour; but it's a certainty that inappropriate, poorly planned teaching will guarantee it, so planning must be the first place you go to when improving behaviour management.

Chapter 7

Reflection and evaluation

For me, evaluating my teaching used to be a subjective business. As the children left the room, I would say, 'Well, I think that went rather well!' or 'Well, they seemed to enjoy it ...'. If I had taught something, quite well in my opinion, to an apparently interested class, then my assumption was that they had learned it. This is still a common equation: *decent teaching plus reasonably co-operative class equals learning*. When asking a question such as 'Why are you sure they all understand right-angled triangles?', I frequently receive the answer, 'Because we did them last week.'

We have said that the most significant driver of your training is the ability to reflect on your work. Brilliant trainees – and teachers – have an embedded habit of reflection. You need to kick-start and develop this habit systematically, exploiting every opportunity for it that your training offers.

The *building blocks of reflective practice* are: a review process based on agreed targets, reflective writing and structured evaluation of critical events. These are all discussed in Chapter 4. Now we must add *your regular evaluation of your own work, especially your teaching*, as discussed below.

The base component of this evaluation is your *analysis of your own lessons*, and this has to go a little further than simple impressions. Subjective evaluation is a start, but on its own it can be misleading. In my own teaching I used to notice discontinuities – for example, the disappointing discrepancy between what seemed to be a lively lesson and a poor written follow-up. Concepts were explained, discussed and illuminated in the lesson, perhaps largely orally (and perhaps with excessive YAVA); but later in the week, when I read the resulting writing, I would be surprised to find that understanding was far less secure than I'd imagined. I was swayed by an active and cheerful session into a subjective but wayward evaluation of the learning, and this may only have been corrected days later. Of course your impression of the lesson is important, but your evaluation can't stop there. Evaluation needs to be swifter, more objective and more explicit than that.

You need to evaluate your own work for two essential and connected purposes – to improve pupil learning, and to improve your own practice. If pupils aren't learning, you need to consider very quickly how to modify your approaches. When things go well, you need to clarify the success for yourself so that you can build on it both in terms of their immediate learning and your continuing development.

Brilliant teachers are evaluating pretty well all of the time, and if this seems a daunting prospect, here are two reassurances. First, you are almost certainly doing a lot more evaluation than you think; and second, it's possible to rationalise evaluation into a straightforward and highly manageable component of lesson planning.

What evaluation isn't

Let's continue to clarify what good evaluation isn't. We've said that it shouldn't be purely impressionistic. Neither is evaluation an afterthought; it is *an essential component of your planning, built into your lesson before you teach it.* So, when you set out your learning objectives, as well as telling yourself about the activities which will support that learning, you should also write down what your evaluation method is going to be. Your standard plan should indicate objectives, activities and evaluation methods for each activity and for the overall lesson.

Similarly, evaluation isn't a complete sweep of every possible lesson issue; it needs to be focused. If allowed to run out of control, it attempts to cover everything – the children's entry into the room, how quickly they settled, whether the weather affected them, whether it was Friday afternoon, how well they responded to questioning, whether they were silent when asked, how much help they needed with the tasks, how noisy they were, whether you talked too much, how well you explained things, how your pace and timing went, how effectively you prepared and used resources ... The problem with such diffuse and ambitious evaluation is that it can obscure the only question that really matters. *Did they achieve the learning objectives?* All other questions are subsidiaries.

Evaluation and assessment

Evaluation isn't a synonym for assessment. Assessment is about pupils' work; evaluation is about your own. Of course, they are connected; the formal and informal assessment of pupils' efforts provides a major indicator of how well you're doing in your teaching. In fact it's a good maxim to repeat to yourself (and, in some circumstances, to your pupils): *If you don't understand this, it's my fault, not yours …*

Parenthesis: some other reasons for assessment

This is an important reason for assessment, but it's not the only one, or even the most obvious. We should consider for a moment the range of things we're doing when we assess, when (for example) we 'mark' children's work. *We mark to keep the bargain* – pupils work for us; we should work for them. This is part of our working contract. *We mark to provide an audience* – so we should always try to engage with the content of pupils' writing, not simply write

assessive comments. The best written comments I've seen extend the writing by asking questions about it, which the pupil may answer – a written dialogue develops around the pupil's work. *We mark to diagnose and begin to correct errors* – so our error correction needs to be focused around clear patterns, reflecting pupil need or current teaching objectives for the class. (There is, of course, no point in correcting all errors. It might make us feel better, but provides no focus or continuity for pupil learning.) *We mark to celebrate pupil talents and successes on which we can build. We mark to gather information about the pupil* which we may need to publish to other people.

But most importantly, *we mark and assess in order to enhance and improve pupils' learning.* We can't plan the journey without a sense of the starting point. There are many creative ways of responding to children's work and your training is bound to describe some of these to you. In choosing among them, you should always remember why you're assessing – especially, that assessment is essential to learning, not a bureaucratic afterthought. The most important assessment is formative.

The information that marking and assessment provide naturally helps us to evaluate the effectiveness of our teaching; but this can be a cumbersome process, and we need to evaluate on a shorter timescale as well. We need to plan the next lesson, or the next stage of the lesson, or the next sentence of our explanation, in the light of how things are going. At least, we need to evaluate the learning before the lesson ends, so that we can modify our plans for tomorrow.

What evaluation is

At its simplest, evaluation is asking and answering the three key questions as your pupils leave the classroom:

1   What were they meant to learn?
2   Did they learn it?
3   How do I know?

Earlier chapters dealt with these. One of the advantages of working always to clear and specific objectives is that you have a way of answering the second two questions, and this is your basis for evaluation.

Three levels of evaluation

It helps to think of evaluation as happening at three levels. At a minimum level, you need to evaluate learning at the end of each lesson. At another level, it is a permanent feature of your teaching. There is, however, a middle way between these which is highly effective and might be a good place to begin creating a semi-formal evaluation practice.

The middle level: evaluating activities

As we said in Chapter 5, the lesson has a progressive narrative. The first activity creates a piece of understanding which, at the transition point, will be discussed explicitly and then developed into a second activity. The transition point, as we've said, is a crucial learning moment. It's also a crucial moment of evaluation.

From poor to brilliant

So you might establish a habit of evaluating learning at each transition point – after each activity. I recently watched a lesson with a middle-ability Year-10 group which was about a scene from *Romeo and Juliet*. In this lesson, the pupils had to understand that the scene that they were reading was very ambiguous. Juliet was saying one thing to her mother but meaning something else, though, cleverly, she wasn't actually lying (and this is a set-up adolescents recognise only too easily). The teacher had quite properly decided that the main objective of the lesson was that pupils would understand the ambiguity of the scene.

A poor lesson would have featured a reading of the scene, alongside which the teacher would have commented on ambiguity and a number of other things as they came up in the text. This lesson was better than that. The teacher had fixed on a main and challenging objective. This immediately raises the focus level of the teaching.

The next thing the teacher had to do was to recognise that this single objective – ambiguity – was actually two objectives. As we've said before, this is so often the case. You can't discuss a particular war of attrition until the pupils know what *attrition* actually means. Weak teaching deals with both objectives – the definition and the application – at the same time, to the detriment of both. Better teaching gives each stage its place and value.

The *Romeo and Juliet* teacher recognised this. She created an opening activity in which *ambiguity* as a term was defined (for example, she compared the word to *ambidextrous*). This was her starter, and she spend five or six minutes on it. Then she invited the pupils to apply this new idea to the text they were studying.

At this point, the lesson started to fail. Even though the teacher had a clear objective and had recognised the appropriate learning stages, the children were largely unable to undertake the main lesson activity, which was to discuss and annotate the text, underlining Juliet's ambiguous statements. They struggled. The concept of ambiguity was too difficult. The teacher eventually stopped the activity and had to put the lesson into the recovery position.

Let's recap what she did well and what she failed to do well. The journey from poor to brilliant could be mapped here as follows:

- *poor:* working through the material, discussing as you go, no learning focus;
- *better:* clear objective to focus understanding;
- *good:* recognising the objectives stages and dealing with them appropriately, perhaps separately;
- *brilliant:* evaluating the learning at transition points and adjusting accordingly.

The teacher here has crossed a number of planning hurdles; she has reached *good* but not *brilliant* in her planning. The main activity still fell apart because, as she closed the starter, she didn't check that pupils understood. They were a quiet, acquiescent class and, perhaps out of courtesy, they gave the impression of understanding what is in fact a subtle and sophisticated concept. (How often do we throw at pupils concepts on which learned books are written by world-class scholars?) In fact, they didn't understand; but because she didn't know this, she moved straight to an activity which they couldn't complete. The starter had a clear objective but the lesson plan allowed for no evaluation of it.

So our structure should be based on explicit evaluation at the end of each activity. We need to know now whether the pupils have any sense of what we mean by culture, or attrition, or congruity. We can't go on to our next activity without being sure of this, and we can't just assume that they've learned it because we've taught it.

How does activity-level evaluation happen?

Before suggesting some specific end-of-activity evaluations, it will be helpful to look again at the *Romeo and Juliet* starter. The teacher had an objective for it (*understand ambiguity*) which is good – you need objectives for each lesson stage. But the *activity* was barely an activity at all. It was in fact more of a *passivity*! It consisted of the teacher explaining to the pupils what *ambiguity* means. The pupils' job was to listen.

The Secondary Framework in the UK favours highly interactive teaching and it's useful to consider what this means in terms of evaluation. Interactivity isn't as obvious as you may think. It's often defined in terms of energy levels and pupil participation. Lots of questions, lots of hands up, lots of felt-tips, lots of noise. These may well indicate interactivity, but they fall short of fully explaining the concept. The teacher has a role here too. The interactive teacher doesn't just set up a lot of activities and ask a lot of questions. The interactive classroom isn't just one where pupils talk a lot; it's one where the teacher *listens* a lot. Interactivity is mutual.

A listening teacher in a lively classroom is on sustained, evaluative alert. Every pupil response provides incidental but powerful evaluative input. In fact additional evaluation activities are probably superfluous. The children are returning their understanding to you at every point and, if you're listening, you are modifying as you go along.

So the least formal, and probably the best, evaluation is the spontaneous evaluation of interactive teaching. But this is highly skilful and demanding, and something you should be hoping eventually to achieve with experience. Meanwhile there is more straightforward and accessible evaluation which needs to become part of your lesson plan, which now has three key components – *learning objective, activity and evaluation.*

So you sketch out in your plan the closing activity which will evaluate the learning. This will be a brief activity, joined more or less seamlessly to the learning activity, or integrated within it. As well as providing you with a snapshot of the learning up to that point it will enable the pupils to sustain and consolidate that learning for themselves. Of course the simplest method is to ask children if they understand but this has limited value. Children usually say they understand, even when they don't; they frankly prefer bewilderment to a repetition of the explanation. (This reminds me of asking for directions when lost in the car. A helpful local gives accurate but complicated directions through the window. After the third turn to the left past the pub I'm completely lost. Why do I keep on pretending I'm following him? Why do I finally say I've got it when I'm nowhere near it?) So try some slightly more elaborate methods:

- They could discuss in pairs a key question about the learning, and then feed back their answers.
- They could give their own created examples – for example, their own euphemisms or their own riddles.
- They could create a one-sentence explanation for other pupils in other classes.
- They could write three key words on their whiteboards.
- They could design their own evaluative questions.
- They could restate the learning objectives in new words.
- They could suggest what the next objective might be.
- They could provide a real-world example of dramatic irony.
- They could explain how this activity related to earlier ones in previous lessons.

Permanent evaluation

You are probably doing a good deal of this already. It doesn't replace the need for evaluation after each activity or, at least, at the end of each lesson. It does require you to be highly sensitive as you monitor reactions in the room.

Almost any classroom activity provides evaluative information and brilliant teachers are permanently susceptible to this. From the first moment of any lesson, you are bombarded with evaluative input. This isn't especially scientific or even systematic; for example, it doesn't always evaluate the learning of every individual; but it's immensely valuable in steering the work. When children are reading aloud, you are checking whether they're understanding what they're reading and reflecting on the appropriateness of the text. When you question the class, you have immediate insight from the nature and frequency of their answers into the appropriateness of the level of work and your explanations so far. Their questions to you signal their comfort level. For example, when you set a task and ask for questions (QDO) and you are faced with a large number of them, you know immediately that your explanation has been unclear and you should stop and re-present it to the whole group. When they're discussing in pairs, you are listening to snippets of discussion; when they're writing, you're looking over their shoulders. When they're feeding back, you're checking their understanding; when they're collaborating with you in a piece of shared writing, you're aware of whether they get the points about the nature of what you're doing. When you're talking to the whole class, you're looking at their faces. The more interactive your teaching becomes, the more frequent and immediate is the evaluation. Literacy Framework starters, for example, model teaching which provides evaluative data minute-by-minute. You aren't just estimating whether they're getting it right; you're estimating whether the teaching is doing its job, is accurately pitched and effectively carried out.

The plenary for end-of-lesson evaluation

The Secondary Framework recognises the value of a final lesson activity which consolidates and evaluates the learning. This is a highly significant and effective component of the Framework lesson, though it is often neglected. Books of starters have been published, but the plenary suffers by comparison. New teachers, for one thing, struggle with timing for two reasons – because it's difficult to estimate how long things will take, and because it's difficult to depart from the lesson script in the middle of a lesson which is clearly over-running. This is a problem which vanishes with experience, but it often leaves in its wake a poor habit of lesson finishing. The plenary quite often disappears in practice; or it is relegated to setting homework and packing up, or to a quick 'What did we learn today?' session, on the bell, the pupils already standing up to leave. At this point, they'll say anything to get out of the room. If the objectives are obvious to them, they'll say they understand them. This is quite possibly meaningless.

Your hour lesson needs a ten-minute plenary (not a five-minute one) and this needs to be a planned activity which will enable you to gauge the mood of the room in terms of your learning objectives, to have a sense at least of the majority achievement, and to consider modifications for tomorrow. Routine is good here, but so is variety; so your plenary activity could be chosen from a list such as this:

- I didn't tell you today's objectives – now, what do you think they were?
- Explain today's learning in one sentence to a specified audience such as your Mum, a seven-year-old child, a class in the year below yours.
- In pairs – what was the most important thing *in your opinion* that you learned today?
- Sum up today's learning in exactly fifteen words.
- In pairs, think up a new (better?) activity to teach today's objective.
- Write an advertisement or a film trailer for today's lesson.
- Write a two-minute radio news story summing up what happened in today's lesson.
- That's the objective – but tell me one other thing you learned today.
- Look back at today's activities – what was the connection?
- Write a newspaper headline for today's lesson.
- Write one more example of your own.
- As a class, complete two columns on the whiteboard headed CLEAR and NOT CLEAR about what we've learned and what still confuses us.
- One thing from today that needs more explanation.
- What do you guess next lesson will be about, and why?
- What does next lesson *need* to be about?

Even suggestions beginning *Write* here are predominantly speaking and listening suggestions. You will emphasise speed here; you will glance at the jottings; you will listen to as many contributions as possible – evaluative plenaries are swift and interactive.

(And then later, if an observer says, 'I don't think they understood what you were saying about trade routes', and you reply, 'Well, I think they did!' and he says, 'Well, how do you know?', you can point to your plenary evaluation and win the argument.)

Some of the later suggestions on this list suggest how a sustained habit of evaluation through plenaries and elsewhere can generate a truly collaborative classroom ethos. Pupils are being invited to drive the learning forward explicitly by considering where it needs to go next. They are participating in evaluation not so much of their own work or of the teacher's efforts but of the learning as a joint operation. The following lesson can in a sense be jointly planned, or at least modified. The teacher can offer her proposed alternatives for tomorrow's lesson and invite comment. The responsibility for the learning is being shared. This doesn't mean, obviously, that the final responsibility isn't yours. If learning isn't secure, or behaviour is not as it should be, you have to consider what you can do about your own practice to improve things rather than simply blaming children for misbehaving or not listening carefully.

Evaluation should provoke two levels of activity for you. In the short (or immediate) term, it might lead you to change the work currently underway with a specific class. In the longer term, it should help you with forward planning and your own development. Table 7.1 shows some judgments and consequent actions which I noted training teachers taking over a period of a few weeks.

In these cases we see teachers using various levels of input to evaluate their work, making immediate modification if necessary and considering their own development. While written outcomes certainly provide rich evaluative material, the more immediate evaluations happen in active and interactive lessons. The more pupil involvement, the more obvious the evaluation. This can be formalised into whole systems of pupil evaluation, where pupils evaluate each other's work and their own. Pupils certainly benefit from systematic evaluation of their own work and brilliant teachers invite this through regular discussion and by encouraging pupils to reflect, perhaps in writing, as a matter of course. Pupil logs can contain progressive personal accounts of developments, problems solved, talents fostered, preferences discovered. As well as benefiting pupils, such logs support all teachers in the continuing task of evaluating and improving their own work.

Table 7.1 Evaluation and action

Input	Evaluation	Short-term action	Long-term action
Children reading Shakespeare aloud badly – stumbling, etc.	Text more challenging than I'd thought; lower understanding than anticipated	More text editing, more active approaches, more checking of learning	More care over text choices; more forward planning re: editing; more DARTs; more checking of understanding
Nearly half the class had questions after task setting	Explanation not as detailed as it needed to be; no QDO	Stopped class, went through instructions more carefully; QDO	Plan instructions, task-setting more elaborately; anticipate pupil problems; test instructions on husband; write out instruction script for self
Disappointing feedbacks after good group discussions	Not enough time and structure given specifically for the feedbacks	Stopped after two feedbacks and encouraged all groups to spend ten more minutes on them	Vary feedbacks; sometimes, no feedback at all; treat feedback as separate task needing its own structure and time
Children inattentive during reading of textbook	Children were bored by text; text is inaccessible for some	Stopped reading after fifteen minutes	Think carefully about choice of texts; vary reading strategies and voices; use shorter reading periods; give focus questions before the reading; QDO (especially O) before reading
Plenary revealed continuing confusion between congruent and similar triangles	Probably compounded confusion by teaching the two together	Stopped lesson and redefined	Don't teach pairs like this! It just seals in the confusion. Teach one or the other in its own context

Chapter 8

Being brilliant

You won't be a brilliant teacher at the start of your training. You can, however, be a brilliant trainee. Before we look at some of the advanced teaching skills that you might aim for in the later stages, let's recap on the qualities that can mark out very promising trainees from the start.

- *Brilliant trainees listen:* resting your own agenda and paying close and generous attention to advice, even if you don't agree with it, marks out a reflective trainee. Being more concerned to defend yourself against criticism than to modify your practice is a certain (and common) barrier to success.
- *Brilliant trainees reflect:* you must drive your own training and this comes predominantly from sustained analysis of your experiences. Every lesson plan should feature your own developmental targets as well as your pupils'; and every lesson evaluation should evaluate your own progress as well as theirs.
- *Brilliant trainees integrate:* it's your job to make sense of all the disparate parts of your training. In particular, don't separate *school* from *university*.
- *Brilliant trainees are more concerned with learning than with teaching:* what matters is that you're clear what pupils are meant to learn and that that (and they) are central to your planning.
- *Brilliant trainees organise:* you are a not a student; you are a professional working within institutions. Being disorganised impacts on colleagues and children; it's no longer an option.

We have covered all these points in earlier chapters. Now it's time to consider in greater detail some of the more challenging skills that you will want to develop in the later stages of your training.

Inclusion and differentiation

As time goes on, your trainers will want you to show a sense of differentiation. They will want your planning and teaching to show that you are aware of the variety within your classroom and that you are making some attempt (for example) to support the least able and challenge the most. This won't happen at the beginning – it depends on experience and advanced skills. But it can develop as your training progresses.

Conscientious teachers feel guilty most of the time. The job is never finished to perfection, the demands can never be fully met; schools are places of permanent compromise; and nowhere is this anxiety more pronounced than in the business of differentiation. It's a matter of common sense that efficient teaching takes account of the varying personalities of those who are learning, but in practical and realistic terms, what are you meant to do? You have twenty-eight pupils with twenty-eight reading ages, personal histories, individual needs, numeracy levels, learning styles, interests, SAT scores, CAT scores, attitudes and preferences, and some of those have changed since last week. And you have four classes a day. They are all mixed-ability classes, because all classes are mixed-ability classes (children don't come in ability-batches of twenty-eight); and a good deal of differentiation isn't just about ability anyway. You need some straightforward and achievable answers to the many complex questions which differentiation asks.

First, stop worrying about it – anxiety is counter-productive; and you are already differentiating a great deal in your teaching. Take stock of what you already do. For example, do you:

- *talk to individuals about their work* in any context? Do you discuss their coursework drafts with them? Do you work on their reading choices in the LRC?
- *always* QDO?
- *give some extra explanation*, perhaps during a QDO session when task setting, or in response to a pupil question?
- *vary class questioning*, for example by avoiding YAVA?
- *give pupils time to discuss tasks in pairs*, perhaps as part of QDO?
- *write comments on children's work*, addressing its strengths, suggesting improvements and developments, and engaging with the content? (See 'Assessment for Learning', later in this chapter.)

- *ask the class questions*, for example, during a plenary, or a lesson transition?
- *answer pupil questions*, and make spaces for them to ask?
- *assess pupils' work?*
- *provide a variety of resources?*
- *use pupils as experts*, for example by allowing them to plan presentations on their own subject enthusiasms?
- *allow peer assessment* from time to time, so that pupils see (or hear) and discuss each other's work? (See 'Assessment for Learning', later in this chapter.)
- *have group discussion?*
- *allow pupils to work in areas of personal interest?*
- *give a choice of tasks* from time to time; for example, allowing groups to choose their feedback method, or allowing individuals to choose their text type (poster, leaflet, newspaper letter)?
- *use a variety of activities* to move towards your learning objectives?

- *explain things two or three ways?*
- *set research homeworks?*
- *set 'family' homeworks,* such as interviewing your mum about her favourite music?
- *chat?*
- *praise?*
- *ask for pupil opinions* on an issue or a text, and perhaps list and discuss those opinions?
- *run interactive starters?*
- *work collaboratively with the whole class,* for example, on a shared writing exercise?
- *work with selected groups,* for example on shared reading?
- *work with Learning Support Assistants,* including briefing and debriefing them?
- *work with computers?*
- *use an interactive whiteboard* for example, to note and print pupil contribution?
- *do pair work?*
- *evaluate learning* and modify your teaching?
- *encourage pupils to keep a subject log?* (See 'Assessment for Learning', later in this chapter.)

You will notice two things about this list. First, although it's a list of differentiation routines, it's also a list of good classroom practices. Good teaching and differentiation are almost synonymous. The second thing is that you can answer 'yes' to many of these questions. You are probably already differentiating on a regular basis. As time goes on you should become increasingly and explicitly aware of your existing differentiation practice. This will help you to build upon it.

There are, of course, well documented categories of differentiation, such as differentiation by *task*, by *outcome*, by *resource*, by *support* and by *response*, and these are partly covered by the list above. Differentiation by *outcome* was for years the standby of many teachers – all pupils will write different essays, even if given the same title – but this is a passive and inadequate approach. Setting a range of *tasks* where pupils choose or are directed to appropriate levels is more robust but, especially as it is likely to combine with the preparation of varied *resources*, this presents enormous practical difficulties to a working or trainee teacher with minimal preparation time. Differentiated *response* may happen spontaneously as you mark work or talk to pupils, but there's nothing particularly systematic about that, and indeed all of these approaches require analysis and careful monitoring. The rewards are great but the demands are significant. It may be that, over a period of time and (ideally) working with other teachers you will prepare some well-resourced and differentiated medium-term plans. As well as providing a range of varied materials and approaches, such a plan needs to consider how they will be targeted and monitored. It's not unusual to see great efforts being made in resource creation undermined by quite crude classroom deployment in terms of who does what and why, often based solely on rough-and-ready notions of ability. You cannot create ambitious, differentiated and targeted work schemes overnight, and, for the sake of your personal sanity and survival, you should attempt this as a long-term project, focusing on one scheme, and working with teachers or fellow-trainees to create central resources.

But in the meanwhile, there are more immediate, achievable and highly effective ways of extending your differentiation repertoire so that your pupils feel valued as individuals with their own access to the curriculum. Consider differentiation by *teacher language*, by *rotation*, by *multiple access* and by *choice*.

Teacher language

How are you making sure that all pupils, whatever their ability, their linguistic competence, their first language, are going to make sense of what you say? Key moments of teacher-talk – explanation and task-setting, for example – need to be presented and re-presented in a variety of alternative ways, using different tones, registers and examples drawn from a variety of contexts. You must plan more than one way of saying and showing key ideas. This isn't difficult, but it needs preparation. You need to use varied language including synonyms, similes, symbols, alternative explanations, ranges of examples and physical modelling if appropriate. Remember that, in explanations, an example is worth a thousand definitions. This differentiated teacher-talk probably won't happen spontaneously; so be prepared to plan, almost to script, key moments.

Rotation

Another simple, uncumbersome approach is that of rotation; this is also available to you without massive planning and resource creation. A couple of years ago I had three extremely able pupils in an 'A'-level group. They were writing essays that could have been published in academic journals, and their conversation in class was extraordinarily analytical and detailed. Of course I was aware that they shouldn't be allowed to dominate the discussion, while at the same time it was clear that less able pupils were benefiting from listening to them. Striking that balance is part of differentiation, and any decent teacher will be thinking about it. In particular, I had to be sure that the three or four pupils who were aiming at D grades didn't feel intimidated, inhibited or undervalued, and that they took part in class activities. I did this by creating discussion activities with clear structure and focus, by judicially altering groupings, by creating tasks which allowed for differentiated responses, and by generating discreetly differentiated research tasks.

However, it became clear to me as I taught the class that a further group of pupils – four bright girls, who in most 'A'-level classes would have been the predominant group – was suffering. They were interested but made little contribution to discussion, and this is vital, since moving the mouth exercises the brain; post-16 teaching is essentially discursive. These very able and conscientious pupils were being overshadowed. I decided to focus on them for about three weeks. I required their inclusion in discussion and I focused my oral and written responses on them. There was a noticeable change in their participation and confidence, though I hope and believe that no one noticed what I was doing.

Differentiation is frightening because of its scale, and this is one simple way to bring it down to size. At any given time, you could be focused on a given sub-group, chosen not necessarily by ability (the girls at the back, the quiet boys, the ones who don't like the topic, the middle row). Members of this group receive the bulk of your spoken and written attention for a week or two, and then you move on. It's not so defined that anyone can notice it; it doesn't exclude others; but it forces you to spread yourself evenly, and it doesn't require you to try to be all things to everybody all the time. This group, which only exists in your mind, is questioned a little more than the others; its answers are responded to a little more than the others; it works with you on guided and shared work a little more than the others; it has its written work marked a little more thoroughly than the others; and then you move on.

Multiple access: inclusion, not segregation

Differentiated teaching provides a multiplicity of access routes to the learning and you can achieve a great deal without graded worksheets and red and blue tables. Think of the learning as a carousel; the pupils climb on from their different points, at different speeds, in different ways. Howard Gardner's concept of *multiple intelligences* (see Chapter 5) is at its simplest a straightforward but very powerful way of dealing with this. Different children understand things in different ways, and the implication of Gardner's list is that we should generate variety in our teaching. We have already seen that variety is central to good teaching, anyway. Gardner's original list is of eight intelligences. It is, however, possible to add to the list. For example, I've found that some pupils understand new ideas when they are set into a story. You could call this *narrative intelligence*.

Table 8.1 Multiple intelligences

Linguistic intelligence ('word smart'):
Logical-mathematical intelligence ('number/reasoning smart')
Spatial intelligence ('picture smart')
Bodily-kinaesthetic intelligence ('body smart')
Musical intelligence ('music smart')
Interpersonal intelligence ('people smart')
Intrapersonal intelligence ('self smart')
Naturalist intelligence ('nature smart')

The point about multiple intelligences is not that you go into preparation overdrive creating eight or nine alternative sets of approaches and dividing the class into learning-style groups, but that you accept *one simple, basic principle* and plan that into your lessons. Consider the key, explicit learning moments; mark them on your plan; they may well occur in transitions; they will deal with the learning objectives. Decide *how you will deal with these key concepts in a variety of ways* which will create a number of access routes. All pupils can deal with all of the alternative routes;

they will work differently for different individuals; they will act as reinforcements of each other for everybody. Multiple access is a natural extension of objectives-based planning. Let's consider an example. This example is from English, but please stay with it even if it's not your subject; it applies throughout. In fact, if you haven't at this moment got a clue about iambic pentameters, my differentiated approach, set out below, should mean that, within a couple of pages, you will have, whatever your subject specialism. That's my learning objective for you. Look at the ways in which I'm trying to teach it; which of them help you to learn? Probably, one of my routes will make the first contact, but it will be supported by some of the other approaches in building your understanding.

My objective, then, is that the pupils, who are studying Shakespeare, will understand the *iambic pentameter*. Iambic pentameter is the line structure that Shakespeare often uses in his plays. It's a ten-syllable line with alternating stress, as in for example:

Once more unto the breach, dear friends, once more ...

A good teacher will pause and explain this metrical device when she thinks it's an appropriate moment but a brilliant teacher will decide that this is a significant piece of new learning, that it needs to become embedded and available for future use (0–24) rather than being cursorily glanced at, and so that it deserves time and a range of approaches.

Consider your own personal preference for taking in new ideas; consider the ways in which you can understand iambic pentameter. Some people will hear it when you repeat a few lines of Shakespeare and point out the pattern, perhaps underlining the stressed syllables, as I have above. Other people will get hold of it when they beat it out on the desk with rulers as drumsticks. Some will count it – five accents, each containing a weak and a strong beat ($5 \times 2 = 10$). Some will value the definition of the words (iamb implies 2, pentameter means 5, the whole means a decasyllabic line of five iambs). Some will chant it, perhaps in groups, either in words or rhythmic sounds (*ti-tum-ti-tum-ti-tum-ti-tum-ti-tum*). Some will make up their own lines (I think I'll go and have a cup of tea ...). Some will see it when you make a diagram of it on the board:

. / . / . / . / . /

Some will like the idea that the rhythm of iambic pentameter resembles a heartbeat. Others will want to compare it to ordinary speech, which, though obviously not as regular, has quite similar ti-_tum_ stress patterns.

There are at least eight different approaches listed above, all drawn from the experience of teaching, not from a need to fulfil Gardner's list, though you will see that they do conform to several of his intelligences. These activities work together in the classroom; _there's no need to segregate them, or the pupils_; they will settle after a time on the combination that makes most sense to them. The teacher focuses on a single clear objective, rather than 'doing' the Shakespeare line-by-line; he provides a rich and varied environment for learning around a defined content focus. For each child, one or two approaches will be central, others will enrich and confirm, others will echo; the combination of analysis and creativity will generate rounded, personal understanding. Differentiation is about synthesis and inclusion, not segregation.

The deployment of this range of approaches is a matter of judgment; you may not use them all; you don't have to stolidly work through a sequence of activities; some of these will be brief additional suggestions. They will often be a simple matter of teacher language rather then of discrete activities. You will monitor and evaluate the learning and call up these approaches as necessary until understanding is secure. The important thing is that you've selected your key objectives and made advance planning notes about the various access possibilities. This is really commonsense teaching, but it's surprising how often teachers don't seem to have alternative routes ready in the background. If a pupil says he doesn't understand, how are you going to rework the learning? Far too often, teachers simply repeat and cajole, raising their voices and talking more slowly like tourists in a foreign land.

In the classroom, this will mean giving twenty minutes, not two, to the learning objective; it may mean covering less ground; it will also mean that your pupils have a chance of genuinely understanding (and so remembering 0–24) the concept.

There are always these alternative routes, and you need to devote a portion of planning time to them. Once you have them, your differentiated teaching will mean that you can move whole classes to higher levels of understanding.

While it's certainly helpful for pupils to think about their own learning preferences, the point here isn't for you to decide on each pupil's learning style and aim certain approaches at him as a result; the point is to offer the variety to everyone; they will naturally fixate on the approaches that work for them. In any case, these learning preferences will change over time; and different approaches will suit different objectives for the same individual.

Choice

I am excited that we now have eleven planets in the solar system – I grew up with nine. I'm glad that Pluto wasn't recently thrown out, though it was demoted to the new category of *minor planet* while two others were actually added. I am not much of a scientist, so why does this matter to me?

It matters because I worked on the solar system in Year 6. At my primary school, we were allowed to choose a topic and research it. Nobody else did the planets, and I've no idea why I chose it – perhaps because I liked science-fiction comics. This was light years ago (well, several decades, anyway) but it remains on quite a shortlist of things I remember from school, because I was allowed to follow an interest and define a way of working. There are opportunities for pupil choice in nearly every lesson (though most are less sustained than my *planets* work was). It can occur at every level of transaction. It can inform the choice of materials to work on – they choose their own sources, their own topics, their own media. They choose whether to make audio tapes or write speeches about climate change. They choose whether to write fiction or something factual about domestic life in the eighteenth century. They choose whether to be for or against the necessity of war. Of course such choices need monitoring, and some children will tend towards easy or repetitive options, so you will need to guide them, but teachers are perfectly able to do that.

I still have a toothbrush that was given to me by a Year-8 girl years ago because I answered a question correctly about dentistry. She had given a fifteen-minute talk to the class and had chosen dentistry because it was her brother's profession. Each member of the class (they could choose to work in pairs) gave one such 'expert' talk every Friday through the year; they had a week to prepare them. One girl brought in her pony. One boy brought in his scrambler motorbike and drove it straight at us up a near-vertical bank. I was frightened at the time, but not as frightened as I am now, when I wake up in the night thinking about it. These were English lessons, but the principle of the pupil-expert, choosing, researching and presenting on subject topics can be applied anywhere in the curriculum. Are your pupils analysing their favourite music, their favourite art? Are they following individual scientific interests?

I also have a piece of work which my daughter did when she was in Year 9. She had no great love for history, but she became fascinated on a family holiday in France by some rough inscriptions made by prisoners on the stone walls of a ruined prison across the road from our hotel. She copied them out and took them home. They were the beginning of an entirely personal scheme of work which she called *Freedom* and for which she read and responded to, among other things, Dickens' *A Tale of Two Cities* and Terry Waite's account of being held hostage, *Taken on Trust*. This was an impressive and sustained effort on her part, and it happened because her English teacher allowed her to follow an enthusiasm and provided support, though the work embraced history and French as well. Brilliant teachers seek out ways of making this possible at some point for everybody. They listen to pupils so that they know what they're capable of. I think it matters very much that, every so often, you sit back and look at your planning and ask yourself where the moments are when children can really develop personal enthusiasms. In the end, as in all aspects of teaching and learning, it must be their momentum, not yours, that carries them through.

We have a chance with differentiation when we stop allowing it to be an anxious, overwhelming grind and recognise it as a spur to a lively, enjoyable, varied, inclusive and active classroom. Perhaps we need to think of it as less of a science and more of an art, at least as creative as it is analytical.

More inclusion: challenging the very able

I was watching a top-set Year 11 history class recently. The trainee teacher was asking them about Mussolini; they were invited to decide whether he was a villain or, alternatively, a victim of circumstances. They were considering various evidence sources to support their judgments. The lesson moved to a whole-class feedback discussion around this question.

I have watched this process often; I've done it myself many times. The teacher takes points on both sides of the discussion. There is an element of creative competition between the two viewpoints and the evidence is being well adduced from the readings. This is going well; but these are very clever children. Inevitably, at some point, one of them says, 'Well, I think he's both.'

The very able often show themselves in this way, by seeming almost to opt out of the teacher's structures. The two or three pupils who refuse to play *victim or villain* are probably not intending to be difficult. What they are doing is signalling to the teacher that he needs to raise his game; the discussion needs to move to a more sophisticated level. In real life, no one is entirely victim or villain; even a dictator is in reality a complex mixture, and these able children have seen that and want to talk about it. This is a wonderful moment in your teaching, reflecting real and subtle engagement from your pupils. How are you to make the best of such an opportunity?

A good teacher (or a brilliant trainee) will be listening for this, and not limited by his own agenda. Such a departure is a movement upwards in terms of thinking skills. He will not be alarmed or offended by it. He will focus on it and invite further explanation and analysis. He will probably invite the whole class to consider this new perception.

These are some of the ways in which we cater for gifted and talented children. We listen carefully to them. We allow them to extend the learning structures, to push at the concepts. We also encourage them to synthesise and compare. As you move into the final stages of training, you should be considering extending the able not just by handing them harder work but by increasingly allowing them to take the initiative.

A creative aspect of this challenge lies in synthesis. Able children are able (and must be encouraged) to make connections; teaching has to move from initial materials into wider contexts. Pupils may come to a preliminary understanding that Mussolini is neither victim nor villain but these concepts are only fully understood when they are extrapolated. Tell the pupils to find other examples of the *victim/ villain* dichotomy – in fiction, in drama, in *Eastenders*, in politics, in the newspapers, in society, away from the lesson, at home, away from the war, away from school. They could research this material for homework and discuss it in class. The single *victim/villain* objective is now being rehearsed into a wide range of contexts. The concept is being roundly explored, and fully understood. It is being abstracted.

To take another example: consider very able pupils understanding the mathematical concept of symmetry from the original lesson outlined in Chapter 5. Imagine some of these pupils now carrying

that single objective into new contexts. From the clarity and focus of that initial, graphical discovery (a whiteboard diagram) they can now find symmetry in paintings, in poetry, in science, in snowflakes, in arguments, in political debate, in music. Imagine a Year-8 pupil able to comment that a particular story or argument isn't very symmetrical. What he has been able to do is to transfer a concept from its origin to a range of new environments. No process better indicates sophisticated and confident understanding.

Differentiation: from C to A

In particular, this able child has been encouraged to move from the *concrete* to the *abstract*. This is a movement that helps us to define and conceive teaching and learning that is inclusive and differentiated. I recently watched some Year-10 pupils analysing holiday brochures in a business studies lesson. They were being asked to consider potential audiences for these brochures which are, of course, essentially advertisements. Quite properly, the teacher had asked them to compare two brochures featuring holidays clearly intended for different markets, remembering that comparing two things is always more than twice as effective as analysing one.

This was a mixed-ability option group and there was a wide range of conversations, which the teacher was managing and prompting very effectively. It occurred to me as I watched that differentiation in the room was happening not via stepped worksheets but by the

high

ABSTRACT

| explicit | analytical | formal | how and why |

HOLIDAY BROCHURE ANALYSIS
What is the primary function?
How does the tone support this function (e.g., reassurance, excitement)
How is the tone achieved (e.g., verb person, sentence lengths)
What techniques are particularly used to sell the holiday?
What is the target audience for the advert?
What other autdiences are there?
Comment on the use of specialist vocabulary
In what ways are the text and pictures related in terms of tone and purpose of the brochure?
Can you see examples of exaggeration or euphemism?

What is the primary function?
Does it work for you?
What's your idea of a perfect holiday?
Which of the two holidays would you choose?
Why did you choose that one?
What could be wrong with the holiday?
Have you ever been on a holiday that wasn't at all like the brochure promised?
Describe a typical day on the brochure holiday
Which of the holidays do you think would be more friendly?
Which of the two holidays is for older people or families?

| implicit | descriptive | personal | what |

CONCRETE

low

teacher's language. In particular, he consistently moved between the concrete and the abstract.

We might consider here some of the topics he covered and the questions he asked.

This was a skilled and experienced teacher; he was deploying these concrete and abstract questions instinctively, moving (apparently) seamlessly between them, not obviously demarking different groups within the room, working with the whole group towards a shared understanding. You will see that he invited concrete thinkers and abstract thinkers to cover similar ground but that the concrete thinkers focused on themselves, their opinions, experiences and reactions, whereas the abstract thinkers were required to be more formally, explicitly and technically analytical of how the brochures worked. The concrete thinkers consider the *what* of the question; the abstract thinkers explore the *how* and the *why*.

You won't be able to think in these terms in your early training, but later it may become possible for you. All you have to do is to look at your planning and consider the discussions you want to run, and the questions you intend to ask. You could ask yourself:

Have I got enough concrete questions to support the less able learners?
Have I got enough abstract questions to challenge the more able learners?

Considering these two questions may lead you to make a few additions to your lesson plan and to (therefore) offering a broader range of opportunities in the classroom. When you start to do this, you are making serious inroads into differentiation.

Meta-learning

In discussing differentiation, we are considering axes along which we can map thinking and learning skills. We have just considered that one fruitful axis runs from concrete to abstract. In fact, any decent lesson could run in that direction; concepts are approached concretely, via example (such as a symmetry diagram on the board); then they are enlarged and abstracted. The more able can pursue the abstraction more fully, generalising the concepts into new contexts and understandings. Another set of higher-order skills concerns how fully children can understand and shape their own learning.

Talented pupils can be extended when teachers allow them access to the learning process. This sounds grand and theoretical, but it's actually a matter of simple common sense. It's also very exciting to watch. Here are some examples of how teachers might do this. I have seen all of these from time to time and, in every case, they have pushed the learning beyond the banal.

- *Instead of publishing the learning objectives on the board at the start of the lesson, they might conduct the lesson and then, at the end, ask the pupils what the objectives were.* In fact, they are inviting the pupils to deconstruct or reverse-engineer the lesson; to work out (perhaps in a plenary pair discussion) why they have been doing what they've been doing; to connect the lesson activities and stages, to see what the running story or theme of the lesson has been. This requires an active and analytical understanding of the learning and high-level synthesis.

- *Instead of presenting the objectives and then setting out the activities, they might inform the pupils of the objectives and then ask them to plan the activities which will be most appropriate.* This would involve pupils in predicting what they thought the teacher was going to ask them to do. For example, a teacher might intend to teach speech marks. His objective is that, in one hour (0–60), the pupils will understand the rules of speech marks. He might inform the pupils of this, and invite them to suggest the best way forward. Some of the pupils suggest the teacher tells them the rules; others suggest that they will find the information in text books; a few suggest (the best idea, and one I've used many times since) that they look at samples of writing which features the correct use of speech marks and work out from that what the rules must be.

- *When setting up the main (centre) lesson activity, they might ask pupils to decide on the connection of this to the just-completed starter activity.* They are inviting pupils to see the lesson journey and perhaps to script the transition, providing the words which the teacher could use to draw out the learning objective from the first activity and transfer it to the next. You might just say, from time to time, 'What's this got to do with what we were doing before?'

- *They might invite pupils to predict aspects of the lesson.* One of the most powerful (but least used) teacher-questions is 'What do you think I'm going to say next?' The most able will be able to predict your thinking; they can see the direction of the learning. Apart from involving pupils, this is an effective form of evaluation. Consider the analytical power of a teacher question like, 'What do you think I'm going to ask you about this?'

For example, a teacher shows children a painting.

- A *competent* teacher may tell them about the painting.
- A *good* teacher may ask them questions about the painting.
- A *brilliant* teacher may ask them what questions they anticipate being asked about the painting, or what questions they themselves would ask about it.

The third variant is brilliant because it requires the children to frame the analysis. It requires them to think not just about the painting but about the whole process of talking about paintings and this is much more significant to the learning than the painting itself.

Inclusion and differentiation: a recap

In the early stages of your training

You won't be able to do much differentiation. Don't worry; but look out for it in your observations, and discuss it with your trainers. As time goes on, use the checklist earlier in this chapter to audit your existing practice and to begin to consider it explicitly.

In the later stages of your training

You should be trying some of the following:

- Varying your language at key lesson moments.
- Offering a range of activities around very clear learning objectives, including occasionally offering choices to pupils.
- Rotating your focus of attention.
- Checking that your questioning covers both abstract and concrete approaches.
- Involving pupils in the planning of the work.

Assessment for Learning

At the start of your training, your thoughts on assessment will focus on marking work and assessing it, often according to assessment criteria such as National Curriculum levels. This is plenty to think about in the early stages. It's also plenty to do; marking work is onerous and usually much less enjoyable than it ought to be. Making sense of pupils' written work in terms of written level descriptions (a process often and rather ominously described as 'levelling') will seem challenging at first. The difficulty will pass with experience. Practise this kind of 'marking' as much as you can; you will over a period reach a stage where accurate assessment (in this sense) becomes instinctive. But right from the start you should try to think about *why* you are assessing pupils' work.

We discussed this briefly in Chapter 7. The process of 'marking' is in fact a complex mixture of activities with a range of functions and processes; it will help if you unpick this, and try to arrive at some underlying principles. Let's consider some of these functions.

As a teacher, you assess to gather information about the standard of pupils' work, perhaps to compare it with national expectations or with other pupils in the school. You may have to publish such information and comparisons to a range of different audiences. Perhaps your colleagues require diagnostic information. Perhaps parents want to know how things are going. Perhaps the government or your employers want to know how your pupils are getting on. Perhaps pupils themselves want to understand their situation.

Apart from this formal assessment practice, which may well involve large-scale and formal processes such as benchmarking and the setting of targets for pupils as an aspect of whole-school policy, there is a range of informal, day-to-day assessment activity, based on activities we still tend to describe rather quaintly as *marking*. As a trainee, it's these *marking* activities that you will be mostly involved with, especially at the beginning. These are vital activities, not simply the building blocks of formal assessment, but arguably of learning itself. If the large-scale activities described above could be called largely *summative*, these smaller-scale marking activities may be though of as largely *formative* (though in fact most assessment procedures have a vital and essential formative element).

In the United Kingdom, there have been interesting developments in assessment, notably within an initiative known as Assessment for Learning (AFL). It's an interesting title, and implies one answer to our earlier question – *why* are we marking? What AFL seems to be telling us is that we don't assess simply in order to gather statistics or to quantify pupils' efforts; we assess (and this includes day-to-day marking) in order to enhance pupil learning. As you progress through your training, you should keep this in mind. When you mark a pupil's work, when (for example) you write a comment or correct an error, you should habitually check yourself: how is this helping his learning?

This isn't as obvious as it sounds. For example, it has implications for your correction of pupils' mistakes. It may be tempting to underline every error, but this is unlikely to focus on patterns or repetitions; nor will it (of itself) provide any remedy. Your job is to explain so that the error is unlikely to be repeated. AFL has implications for written comments, too. In fact you might like to think of written comments as working at three levels – *assessive*, *developmental* and *engaged*.

An *assessive* comment makes a quality judgment, as in:

> Very good work, though the arguments about the role of Guy Fawkes are quite weak.

I see this kind of comment frequently. In terms of our single criterion – does it enhance learning? – it isn't wholly useless. It draws attention to what needs improving, though it offers no suggestion as to how it should be done.

A *developmental* comment builds on this:

> Very good work, though the arguments about the role of Guy Fawkes are quite weak. You should consider what Johnson says and compare Fawkes' role with some of the other conspirators.

It's obvious that this is more enhancing. It offers practical suggestions for improvement. As you move through your training, you should certainly be offering developmental feedback like this, orally and in writing. However, a strong teacher (and a brilliant trainee in the later stages of training) could graduate to the third, *engaged* level:

> Very good work, though the arguments about the role of Guy Fawkes are quite weak. You should consider what Johnson says

and compare Fawkes' role with some of the other conspirators. How would you have changed the punishments given out?

Here you are actually involving the yourself in the pupil's writing, offering a dialogue with him. I've seen this in pupils' work books – the teacher writes a question arising from the work, and the pupil writes a reply. Such a dialogue isn't common, but when it happens it can become more enhancing that the original piece of work.

This isn't only fuller and more helpful – it's actually different in kind to the other comments, because it involves itself with the content of the pupil's writing; it engages with his thought. This engagement, which can also be achieved orally by teacher response to discussion, is significant in several ways. It builds a relationship in which the teacher is much more than an assessor and the pupil (therefore) much more than a passive recipient of knowledge and judgment. It differentiates, of course. Most of all, it seeks to engage the pupil by respecting his opinions and contributions. This is likely to enhance and extend the pupil's learning.

It's also a predominantly positive comment. Consider your comments, or consider the three sample comments above. The first is mostly negative; the second is about half negative; the third is largely positive. Are you achieving at least parity between what the pupil will perceive as negative and positive? And do remember that what may be intended as developmental support can look very like criticism to an adolescent. You aren't an adolescent, but don't you (even so) get tired of feedback which only focuses on weaknesses or 'development areas'? Celebrating positive achievement ('I particularly like the way you …') and commenting explicitly on progress ('You are far better now at …') is not only good for morale and relationships but efficient in defining and building improvement in your pupils. All of this may seem fairly obvious, but in reality many teachers stop at the assessive or developmental level in their marking and it does seem to need a conscious effort to habitually move beyond it. Of course, it requires more work and you haven't time to always do it for everybody; but you could combine it with *differentiation by rotation*, as discussed earlier in this chapter.

We are making the point that assessment drives learning. We don't mean that tests set the agenda for the classroom; we mean that we plan appropriate lessons when we know what pupils are good at and what they need to do better. This is what your mentor does for you when she watches you teach; she tells you what went well, and sets targets to improve what didn't.

It's worth reflecting on this simple *strengths/weaknesses* model. People are quite uncomfortable with the *weaknesses* part of it and usually rename *weaknesses* as *areas for development* or some such euphemism. I think we are right to be wary of this simple dichotomy but I don't think that the problem is solved by rebranding it.

The problem with *strengths/weaknesses* as a comment model is that it's not as balanced as it looks. *Weaknesses* is the stronger partner. Even if the teacher (or your mentor, giving feedback to you) is fastidious about half-and-half, the pupil is likely to remember and react to the weaknesses. The criticisms bother us disproportionately; that's human nature. For us to feel complimented we need about 80 per cent positive feedback.

However, the problem goes deeper than pupil reaction and morale. Ultimately, the problem is that weakness preoccupies the teacher as well as the pupil. Consider comments at the developmental level. The most common formula is:

> You are good at A, but not so good at B. We must now work on B in the following ways ...

Of course, this is common sense, and often it's the right direction. Assessment is driving learning. But the AFL relationship doesn't have to be negative, and progression is unbalanced if it always is. How often do you see comments like this?

> You are good at A, but not so good at B. We will work on B later, but for the moment we will build on the strength that you have with A ...

The AFL relationship demands that you build on strengths as well as remedying weaknesses. The pupil works particularly well with historical sources, or has a very strong sense of how to apply algebra to real life, or is advanced in the technical analysis of poetry or the grammar of German. It matters very much to the pupil's development (not just to his morale) that these individual abilities are recognised and extended in your marking and the planning that flows from it. In this way your work is strongly differentiated and is likely to take pupils to new levels of sophistication within areas of strength. *To sum up: they need to move forward in areas of strength as well as areas of weakness.*

There is in fact a wide range of assessment practice, and a brilliant trainee in the later stages of training will be moving well beyond 'marking'. For example, there is self-assessment. You may encourage pupils to keep logs of their own experiences in your subject, perhaps writing responses to your marking comments, setting themselves targets to address as a result, marking and reflecting on their own work. A very interesting practice is to have the pupil mark her own work first. She may grade it according to relevant criteria (which have been explained to the whole class) and she will comment on its strengths and weaknesses. Then she will submit it for teacher-marking, without her grade or comments. Later she will be able to compare her marking with yours.

Peer marking can be used on its own or combined with other processes such as self-marking or teacher-marking. Pupils need to be given clear criteria for marking each other's work, and to be reminded about positivity and development. It's certainly true that they will find things to say that teachers don't. Some research indicates that pupils will in fact be more critical than teachers are. This is also certainly true of self assessment (and this includes the self-assessment of trainee teachers who, when reflecting on their teaching, are usually their own severest critics). So it's clear that a range of assessment types is likely to provide rich, varied and balanced information. As you progress in your training, you will extend your assessment repertoire. But you must remember always its fundamental purpose, its fundamental connection with learning. You begin your lesson planning by knowing what pupils are good at and where they need to go next.

Assessment for Learning: a recap

In the early stages of your training

You will mark pupils' work and you will 'level' it against Key Stage 3 criteria. As time goes on, you will also work with GCSE and post-16 criteria. You will try to be positive and developmental in your comments.

In the later stages of your training

You will extend your assessment repertoire and try some peer- or self-assessment. You will find out about and contribute to school assessment policies. You will try to be positive, developmental and engaged in your comments. You will link assessment to learning by using assessment information to clarify strengths and weaknesses, both of which will inform your planning.

You can see from these recaps that being brilliant can be formulated. It's important, especially in the later stages of your training, to return to these concepts of inclusion and AFL because they will sustain and reinforce your development, furnishing you with clear routes to excellent practice in your training and your later career.

Chapter 9

Finishing and starting

Like a wedding, the culmination of months of preparation, completing your formal training is a beginning rather than an end. What matters most is that you carry forward into your first post a momentum of development.

In the UK, your training continues in effect into at least your first year of teaching. This might seem a dispiriting notion; you have passed your driving test but now apparently have to wear those obnoxious green P-plates for months to come. However, you should try to see the induction in positive terms. It is likely to offer you various perks. You will have a reduced timetable as well as a programme of support within your first school. A well-run induction should make you the envy of your colleagues, so take advantage of it while you can.

Career entry

You are likely to have to prepare a form of Career Development and Entry profile in the final weeks of your teaching. In the UK, current details of this may be found at the web site of the Training and Development Agency which is listed in Chapter 1 (http://www.tda.gov.uk/teachers/induction/cedp.aspx). It is a compulsory feature of your training, a document that you will carry from your training to your first school, and its audience is the senior colleague who will oversee your induction support. Keep this (as yet unknown) reader in mind as you complete it.

Preparing a profile is fairly straightforward. It will be especially easy if you have maintained a reflective journal or profile throughout your training, where (for example) you have assembled evidence for the achievement of skills and the achievement of competencies such as (in the UK) the QTS Standards. If you have been in the habit of writing reflectively about your strengths and weaknesses, and discussing them developmentally with your trainers, you will be well placed to take from that reflection some key focuses for your continued improvement. Brilliant teachers continue to change throughout their careers. You don't leave your training with a finished practice which will always work, and teachers who think that way are bound to fail eventually. There are many new teaching environments waiting for you out there that you haven't even guessed at; you will have to keep changing and growing. After fifteen years in teaching, you need to have had fifteen years' experience, not one year's experience fifteen times. This isn't pious idealism; it's simple necessity. One way in which you can begin to take control of this process is to prepare a useful Entry Profile. Even if you're not required to, you should make one anyway, because it will empower you in the immediate future, and empowerment, when you're a first-year teacher, isn't easily come by. Remember that the statements the profile makes about you are likely to be countersigned by your trainers and so should carry some authority.

Virtually any Entry Profile is likely to fit a *strengths-and-weaknesses* pattern (though, as we said in the previous chapter, *weakness* isn't a term that's often used). One important thing to remember here is that, from a practical point of view, the *weaknesses* section (we'll call it the *Development Targets* section from now on) is probably the more powerful. Of course you will want to prepare a statement about what you've handled particularly well. This will support you in various ways. If you have been especially good at sixth-form teaching, for example, a profile statement to that effect, signed by your trainers as well as by you, may help you in negotiating access to this on your timetable. So in choosing strengths to include in your profile, remember the practical use to which the profile will be put. General statements of strength (*jolly good at lesson planning*) are of some value in establishing your credentials in your new job but aren't going to be as helpful to your ambitions as specific indicators of expertise or enthusiasm.

For this reason, the *Development Targets* section is likely to be particularly helpful. This is where you (in effect) write yourself tickets for future support, training and experience. Don't bother stating the obvious. You may well need more experience of assessment, or of pastoral work, but (believe me) you're going to get that anyway, in abundance! Training costs money, and you need your profile to support you when you apply for it, when you may be in competition with other teachers. If your profile says you need more experience of drama, or biology, or swimming, that will support you when you seek additional training. This is one of the Induction perks that we mentioned earlier.

So, to summarise: be sure to include specifics within the profile, and don't be diffident about listing Development Targets. They aren't confessions of failure, but rather requests for specific further experience. Above all, remember whom you're writing for and what you want to achieve.

The induction period

As we've said, be thankful for induction. It means that somebody is committed to support your continued development within your first school. It probably confers a few privileges on you to underwrite this. In the UK, the induction period – the first year of teaching – is likely to include provision such as:

* an individual programme of support within your school, to ensure that you meet the appropriate teaching Standards, organised by your induction tutor;
* observation of and feedback on your teaching;
* a timetable no greater than 90 per cent of a full teaching timetable;
* your own observation of experienced teachers;
* other professional development opportunities (for example, access to training courses, and regular in-school policy induction), often based on the Entry Profile;
* some funding paid to your school to underwrite your induction.

Most (but not quite all) schools can undertake induction for NQTs (newly qualified teachers). Those categories of school that can't are listed on the TDA web site. Obviously, you will want your first post to be in a school which is not only licensed to conduct induction but which has a good programme in place. At interview (in that awful moment when they ask you if you have any questions) you should enquire about the specifics of their programme. Beware of vague generalisations. A good induction practice implies a school which supports its staff not only through induction, but beyond it.

This might sound to you as though training, which you had fervently hoped to be coming to an end, is in fact infinite. Keeping a file of evidence of Standards met, being observed and fed back to, having regular meetings with your tutor, may sound all too depressingly familiar. Cheer up! Although there is (as we've said) a sense in which your professional development is continual, your initial training is over. NQT stands for newly *qualified* teacher; you are fledged and employed, with a salary, some autonomy, and no more professional obligations than anybody else. Use your induction; don't let it use you.

In fact, NQTs are generally happy with their status. Schools are too busy for them to be treated with kid gloves; they certainly are plunged into real teaching and don't feel marginalised. At the same time, they enjoy the continued training, which often begins to feed into formal and accredited professional development at master's level. A strong induction programme lends real impetus to their careers.

Choosing a school

Before you even start reading the job advertisements, you should make a list of criteria for your first job. It's too easy to drift into a first post and then to regret it at length. Teaching interviews (more on this later) typically take up one day, and the job is offered at the end of it. You have no time to consider the offer; you must accept or reject before you go home; so you have to do everything you can to be sure you're making the right decision.

This process starts with clarification of the sort of school you want. As well as geographical area, consider questions such as:

- can you work in a single-sex school?
- do you want to work at a high academic level?
- do you really want an independent school?
- do you want to improve the lives of disadvantaged children?
- does size matter?
- is your subject the most important thing?
- must you have a sixth form?
- must you have younger pupils?
- what curricular features must you have?
- what sort of ethos suits you?
- do you like system and routine?
- do you prefer creative chaos?

Some of these issues might not matter. In fact, a very good first step would be to take the above list, add to it any further questions of your own, and then arrange it in order of priority, with *must-haves* at the top, and *less-importants* lower down.

Let's consider the matter of *ethos* in a little more detail. It's an over-used word. Technically, it relates to the word *ethic* and so refers to the governing ethical codes and attitudes of the school. Thus, a Roman Catholic school has a formally defined Catholic ethos. However, the term is used more loosely (and quite usefully) to define the prevailing atmosphere and aspirations of a school community. It's important that you try to define for yourself the sort of ethos in which you can work. You could start by thinking about your various placement schools and the differences between them. Where were you happiest? Why?

Here are a couple of stereotypes. Like all stereotypes, they are simplified and irritating, but not pointless. Suez Street High is in a deprived area of a big city. It has no sixth form. It has been in special measures, but is now emerging. Its reputation remains poor, and it isn't the school of choice in the city. The children are challenging. A community police officer visits the school often and has his own desk in the foyer. Examination results are poor. There is an extensive whole-school behaviour management policy. St Sycamore's, on the other hand, is just outside the city boundary. Exam results are well above the national average; pupils behave very well; there is a thriving sixth form, many of whom drive better cars than the teachers. People move house to get their children accepted.

These are comic-strip perceptions but they have some limited base in reality. Certainly the prejudices behind them do. One of your first decisions must be about which type of school you're looking for. It's not uncommon for trainees, rightly full of idealism, to feel almost obliged to opt for Suez Street. They feel they should – it's a moral obligation. And then there are trainees who go for St Sycamore's because they think it will be easier to work in. Neither of these is a sufficient, accurate or lasting reason. Look at your assumptions, question them, and be honest with yourself. This is a job as well as a vocation, and you will live with this decision on a daily basis for years. Be personally clear about what you're good at and what you're looking for. It's perfectly all right (for example) to go for St Sycamore's if that's the kind of challenge you want. And it's far better to avoid Suez Street than to opt for it for unrealistic reasons. They want practical teachers there, not missionaries.

Beyond the caricatures, there are advantages and challenges in both schools. Suez Street will tire you; it will present behaviour management challenges on a daily basis. But it may well have a strong staff with well-developed support mechanisms. It probably won't leave you to fend for yourself. It may well have a strong focus on teaching-and-learning policies, because it has to – it can't survive on lazy teaching. Relationships made there may be hard won but particularly rewarding. There may well be a great deal of energy within that school devoted to making it better and improving its local standing. There may be a sense of moving forward. You will learn a lot, and be strengthened by the experience.

St Sycamore's won't make those demands. But the children won't be perfect, and the behaviour policies may be less supportive. There may be less interest in teaching-and-learning policies because, well, it just seems to work as it is. There may be complacency. At the same time, there may also be a great deal of academic pressure on you from senior staff and parents – the exam results matter very much here, and it's possible for this to have a stultifying effect on imaginative teaching. Nevertheless, you will be able to operate at a high academic level and you won't spend your life worrying about discipline.

The point is not to make choices for the wrong reasons. The right reasons begin with clear and honest self-knowledge. Once you've established that, you move on to critically assessing what's available. You shouldn't be asking 'Is it a good school?' You should be asking, 'Is it the right school for me?'

While it's a good idea to send your CV to local schools that interest you, your first contact will normally be through advertisements and the job descriptions ('blurbs') that follow your initial enquiry. Do remember that these are advertisements and it's not a bad idea to read them as critically as you would a leaflet on double-glazing. Look for what they don't tell you as well as what they do – no mention of exam results? No mention of induction or staff support? Look for telling phrases such as *special measures* or *improving* and consider what they really mean. Read this material forensically, but above all read it with a clear sense of what you're looking for. Remember: even the job description is an advert.

Having decided that you're interested in a school, you need to find out more about it. This will help you to decide whether to apply, obviously; but it will also help you to make your application appropriate and attractive. You should start with the Ofsted web site (http://www.ofsted.gov.uk) and read the school's report, or at least a summary of it. There will be a section on your subject department. Look for signs of improvement and indications of good management. But do remember that teachers are sceptical about Ofsted and the whole story of the school isn't to be found there. Indeed, if there are Ofsted issues that concern you, but you still attend for interview, you can raise them as questions.

How else do you find out about the school? Talk to people who went there or who work there. Go to the local pub and ask the bar staff. All accounts are partial, so gather as many as you can. But remember that school reputations are like oil tankers; they take a long time to turn around. A school which is making great improvements may carry its poor reputation for some years.

Finally, therefore, you have to trust your own judgment and your own observations. On interview day, you will be occupied in many ways; it's not the best time to be making your own decisions. One way out of this dilemma is to arrange a *preliminary visit*. Most schools will accept this arrangement; some will even offer it. You can telephone and arrange to meet the subject leader or other staff and have a look round. This is beneficial in several ways. For one thing, it creates a favourable impression of you as conscientious, committed and having initiative. And it gives you a chance to have a good look at the school and the children.

This looking is crucial. It will happen on a preliminary visit and on interview day. Remember above all that what you're looking at is people and their relationships. There may be a lovely all-weather pitch, a fabulous ICT suite or a brand-new drama studio. Without the right staff and pupils, such facilities are useless.

How do you get to see pupils? Arrive early, so you have to wait. Get lost and ask the way – how do the children respond? Look at the graffiti – how much is there, where is it, what does it say? What does this tell you about the school community and its relationships? If offered lunch with the pupils, accept. Lunch may be where the ethos of the school most clearly announces itself. It's no accident that ancient independent schools (and universities) have the most elaborate meal time rituals. They know that this is a powerful way of establishing the culture of the place. How orderly, how supervised are the lunch arrangements?

Similarly, get into the corridors. The classrooms belong to the teachers; the outside areas belong to the children; but the corridors are no-man's-land, the ambiguous interface between kids and adults, and so extremely revealing about that relationship. How polite, caring and systematic is corridor life? How loud is it?

Remember, we're not talking here about good and bad as absolutes. I'm not saying that order is good and noise is bad. That's your decision, and you've already made it before you set foot in the school.

Selling yourself

For many, this isn't an easy concept. You can go too far, or not far enough; but you do have to remember that the process of getting a job involves self-advertisement at every stage. You need to convince people of your worth without alienating them by being over-boastful. This balance can be achieved, but it needs thinking about.

A good starting point is to list your virtues. There are three possible elements here: your generic virtues, as an NQT; virtues specific to yourself; and virtues that apply specifically to the job in question.

Let's consider your *virtues as an NQT*. You are probably applying for a job that advertises itself as appropriate for new teachers and it's helpful to consider why any employer might want to state this preference. Believe it or not, NQTs as a group are attractive, for at least two reasons. First, they are cheap. Second, they are still learning and are likely to fit well into a team. They can be moulded.

This is a significant asset. There's nothing sinister about it. A subject leader often sees an NQT as someone with few preconceptions of how schools and departments should run, someone who will adapt to prevailing teaching styles, who can be shaped to fit the space. This gives you an advantage over a competitor with a couple of years' experience who thinks she knows all about the profession. You need to emphasise your flexibility at every stage of the process. Your application letter, for example (which we will discuss further later on) needs to confirm that you are aware that you are still learning the job and that you are looking for a school that will continue to build you as a teacher. This is a good way to close your letter. It's reassuring to a potential employer. By the same token, you should avoid overly assertive generalisations of educational philosophy. You don't yet know everything about teaching and learning and should avoid making dogmatic statements.

Next, you should consider *virtues specific to yourself*. Leona wasn't getting interviews, so I looked at her application letter. She had been a paediatric nurse for about ten years before training as a teacher. She mentioned this briefly in her sixth paragraph. We had a discussion about how that nursing experience related to teaching (working with children, understanding their development, working in a team, working in a public-service environment, taking responsibility – the list was very long). She rewrote this section and repositioned it as the second paragraph. The interviews started. You need to list all experiences and qualities that relate in any way to teaching and to make notes on how transferable those skills are. This then feeds into your letter and your interview. And you need to consider very carefully the sequencing of your letter and CV. It doesn't have to be chronological. It needs to relate to the selling purpose of your application; the strong points need to come early, not to be buried.

Finally, obviously, you should consider the *job description* and be clear how it relates to your strengths. Look for particular curricular or extra-curricular requirements and be sure to mention these in your letter. But be honest – don't make promises or commitments you can't honour.

The power of specificity

So, you are approaching your application with a clear sense of your own worth. How do you combine this with the need to avoid seeming like a know-all? The answer lies in one simple concept – *be specific*. Show me, don't just tell me. What anyone talking to you or reading your letter wants is access to your teaching personality. What sort of teacher are you, and what sort of teacher do you want to become? The problem with such (deceptively simple) questions is that they tend to provoke generalised answers such as:

- I'm very committed;
- I'm enthusiastic;
- I will give 110 per cent;
- I want to be firm and friendly;
- I want every child to achieve his or her full potential;
- I believe in a differentiated approach;
- my classroom is very interactive; and so on.

Some of these may be working towards a genuine self-description but they could all be described as pious generalisations. They are clichés. One way of testing such statements is to consider whether any of your fellow-candidates would say anything different. An enjoyable variant of that approach is to reverse the statements. If the opposite of the statement is ridiculous, then the statement itself is probably not worth making. Consider these opposites:

- I'm not very committed;
- I'm lethargic;
- I will give about 60 per cent;
- I want to be firm and unfriendly;
- I want kids to achieve about half of their potential;
- I teach everybody the same;
- my classroom isn't interactive, really...

Of course you wouldn't dream of saying any of this; so are you making any seriously defining statement about yourself when you generalise?

You avoid all this by being specific. In your letter, and your interview preparation, define several aspects of your teaching so far, during your training, that have been successful and that illustrate you working as a teacher. Instead of:

> I am very committed and enthusiastic. Teaching is so important because children are the future and deserve the best preparation for life, which includes lively and varied teaching through preparation, good learning objectives and appropriate resources ... (etc.)

(try the *opposites test* on that!) try:

> I particularly enjoyed my drama work with Year 8. I was new to drama and I was fascinated by the pupils' responses. We created a village project, with role-cards for all the villagers, and ran a series of village-hall meetings about the building of a ring road. I learned a good deal from this, including that good behaviour comes from well-planned and structured work. The pupils became very involved in their roles ...

The second paragraph is moving me towards a genuine picture of a teacher at work. It shows (rather than just telling) positive things about that teacher's practice but the specifics of it help it to avoid pomposity. This is someone who reflects and is still learning. I can work with her.

Getting the interview

Your application will consist of a an application form or a CV and a letter of application or personal statement. To summarise:

- make the application specific to the job;
- remember that the CV is an advertisement as well as a collection of data;
- remember that the letter/statement is an advertisement ;
- think carefully about the sequencing of the CV and the letter/ statement;
- don't be pompous;
- avoid generalisations and clichés;
- be specific;
- show me, don't tell me (use examples to show your strengths);
- be flexible;
- be reflective;
- be open to further guidance.

Winning the interview

Prepare for your interview

You may well have to teach a *show lesson* (see below) and it's common for this to dominate your preparation. In fact the *formal interview* (which is usually with a panel, including school governors, and often takes place in the afternoon) is a major decider of whether you get the job. You need to prepare for it.

You do this by practising, obviously. Ask colleagues, friends, placement-school staff to interview and to give you feedback afterwards. But you need also to practise answering questions. It doesn't really matter what the practice questions are: take a list of them, go into a quiet room, and rehearse some answers out loud. Here are some sample questions, gathered from trainees over the last few years:

- What do you read for pleasure?
- Do you approve of the National Curriculum?
- Should teaching be more vocational?
- What's the dullest part of your subject?
- How would you make that more interesting?
- Tell me about the best teaching you've done so far.
- Why was it so good?
- What's the worst part of a teacher's job?
- If you disagree with the subject leader's instructions, what do you do?
- What sort of reputation do you want to have among the children?
- What would your classroom look like?
- What department responsibilities could you take on?
- What's your weakness?
- How do you control a difficult class on Friday afternoon?
- What are your strengths as a teacher?
- What do you most need to learn?

You may in reality be asked all or none of these questions, but you need to practise answering them. You need also to look at the quality press in the week of your interview. There's always a news story about education (exams are getting easier/exams are being changed/playing fields are being sold off/Shakespeare is being axed, etc.) and you should have a view about it.

What's a good answer?

'Just relax, enjoy it, and be yourself ...'. As interview advice this is as hilarious as it is useless. You can't, and probably shouldn't, *relax*. You may possibly *enjoy* the interview (it does happen and is usually a good sign) but you can't set out to do so: that's beyond your control. And *'be yourself'* is meaningless. You have many selves already; your teaching self (or selves – you have several) is not your wife or father self; and your interview self is yet another variation. So you need to cultivate a teaching-interview personality which is not false but which reflects your most appropriate characteristics.

Listen carefully to questions. It's fine to ask for clarifications. It's fine to pause briefly to think before answering. It's fine to turn back to the original questioner and say, 'Have I answered your question?' *Offer balanced answers*. It's a conversation, so feel free to take it forward yourself, using examples from your own experience. If you feel a country-and-western moment coming on ('children are the future ...') switch quickly to a relevant account of success from your own teaching. Analyse the success ('I think it went well because...') as well as describing it. Stay specific. Don't talk too much, but don't just answer questions. The best interview will have more of you and less of them. Brief answers to detailed questions may be accurate and succinct but they aren't creating a picture of you. Stick to the point, however. Look them in the eye (and move this around the group of interviewers, don't fixate on one) but don't stare manically. Be positive. You may have legitimate and analytical negative things to say ('I didn't enjoy my second placement, the department was very disorganised ...') but the danger is that you will be remembered as a complainer, someone who passes the blame on to others – not great as a colleague.

Some questions come up so often that it's worth thinking them through beforehand. A favourite is 'What's your weakness?' and the trick, of course, is an honest answer that isn't too damning. The one I've heard most, and which I personally find most loathsome, is 'Well ... I'm a perfectionist.' If ever an answer were prepared to present a strength thinly disguised as a weakness, this is it. Not only is it obvious, but the sentiment itself is highly unpromising. Schools are places for idealists, but not perfectionists; nothing in school is ever finished (the literal meaning of *perfect*, by the way) or as good as it could be; schools are places of eternal compromise, and self-styled perfectionists are often those colleagues who moan about everything not being exactly as they would like. Remember the idea of the *balanced* answer. My own (entirely truthful) answer to this is, 'I have good ideas but I'm not so good at seeing them through. I'm a better starter than finisher.'

Another predictable question will concern behaviour management. What are your interviewers looking for? It's easy to think about the entire process in terms of a sort of talent competition; the winner will be the most deserving candidate. Though there's some truth in this, it's better to think in terms of appropriateness. Your interviewers aren't dispassionate judges who select the best person, award a prize and disappear. They will have to work with you, some of them quite closely, every day for some years. In these terms, what would you be wanting from a new employee?

* someone who you can have a conversation with;
* someone with a sense of perspective (and thus humour);
* someone who will listen;
* someone who will properly discuss issues with you if they disagree with you;
* someone who is positive;
* someone who will take direction and guidance and work in the team;
* someone (however) who can get on with the job independently;
* someone professional;
* someone who isn't going to be a problem.

In connection with this last point, interviewers know how problematic behaviour management can be for NQTs and how much time can be taken up if this goes wrong. They are likely to ask you questions about it. Remember, every single candidate is capable of generalised statements about low-key management, intrinsic management, following school policies, positivity and so on. There's nothing wrong with any of this material, but your competitors have all got it too. What haven't they got? By definition, they haven't got your personal experience of teaching a particular class which presented problems and finding a way of dealing with that which allowed you to reflect and draw some conclusions about how this is done. Tell the story and analyse its lessons. This is memorable, and it will allow you to talk positively, reflectively and enthusiastically.

The show lesson

Some years ago, somebody noticed that interviews had limitations when it came to selecting teachers. They tended to favour people who were good at interviews rather than people who were good at teaching. And so the *show lesson* was born. In quite a short time, it has become an established feature of the selection process.

The lesson can run from twenty to sixty minutes. It usually centres on a theme or piece of content provided by the school. You will receive information when you're invited for interview. You will be told, for example, the age-range and ability-level of the class. On the day, you will arrive ready to do your piece of teaching as well as to undergo your formal interview.

In preparing your show lesson, you should consider why you're doing it and what your interviewers are looking for. Having spoken to many interviewers and interviewees, it seems to me that the criteria are few and simple. They want to see that you can stand in front of children and make good contact with them; that you can prepare straightforward and focused learning activities; that you have some appropriate subject knowledge; and that you can reflect thoughtfully on your own teaching. These issues are the point of the show lesson, and you should consider their implications for your planning.

First, you need to show that you can *make quick working relationships with children*. You must therefore plan your lesson to show that you can talk effectively to them (but not for too long – remember the three-minute rule) and that you can listen to them, engaging with what they say. So a good show lesson begins with some fairly brief and focused introduction, which will probably involve setting an initial task, or running a brisk question-and-answer. Children need to be talking to you within three minutes. If you gather answers from the class, use a whiteboard to list them.

What you don't need here is to be weighed down with resources. You don't want to be handing out dozens of worksheets or other materials. You don't want to be depending on the dubious compatibility of electronic equipment. You don't want to be writing notes on a whiteboard at enormous length with your back to the class. The main theme of all your preparations is this: *keep it simple*.

As we've already said, behaviour management is a big issue when selecting new teachers. The class in front of you will not be a difficult one (that would be logical but cruel) but you should be sure to show low-key skills. For example, don't YAVA; bring in non-participants by directing questions at them, so that you're building a sense of inclusion. Keep the pace brisk and the mood friendly, but don't rush. Don't try to pack an hour into twenty minutes. It matters more that you move at your natural pace than that you get through everything. Be watching and gently monitoring the class rather than fussing with piles of over-complex resources or confusing multiple task-setting. There should, of course, be some variety in what you do. A twenty-minute show lesson should feature around three different class activities, but not six. Don't over-plan.

Your *planning* should show that you plan from objectives rather than activities. Your show lesson should be based around one or two very specific learning objectives. Don't be afraid to reduce and particularise any learning aims which you've been given. For example, if you're told that the children should learn about poetic techniques, be sure to rewrite that objective naming and listing the precise techniques (and not too many of them) that you will be focused on. Be sure that your activities relate absolutely clearly to those objectives. Probably, you should briefly share the objectives with the children near the beginning.

You should take the chance to show your evaluative practice as well. You might check what children already know about the topic (this could be your opening q and a) and your closing activity could in fact be a sort of brief, evaluative plenary.

How is the show lesson integrated into the interview?

You might reasonably assume that your observers:

* will ask you about the lesson;
* will question your planning decisions;
* will ask whether you were happy with the lesson and how you might change it;
* will ask how you evaluated or would evaluate the learning;
* will ask what lessons might follow, or what homework you might set; and so on.

In practice, it seems that such questions aren't always asked. It's not uncommon for the show lesson never to be mentioned again. However, you would be adopting a risky policy if you didn't anticipate all of these questions in your preparation.

In summary, one or two themes run through the whole business of moving from training to teaching. See it as a continuum. Make it work for you. Be honest with yourself; and be specific when you can. The training, which may have seemed lengthy in prospect, and never-ending at times, will be over suddenly. You may even miss it; but you now have the prospect of the most frustrating, exhausting, creative and rewarding career as a brilliant teacher.

Suggested reading

Black, P. and Wiliam, D.: *Inside the Black Box* (Nelson)
Bruner, J: *Towards a Theory of Instruction* (Norton)
Capel, S. Leask, M. and Turner, T.: *Learning to Teach in the Secondary School* (Routledge)
Clarke, S.: *Formative Assessment in the Secondary Classroom* (Hodder)
Ginnis, P.: *The Teacher's Toolkit* (Crown House)
Kyriacou, C.: *Essential Teaching Skills* (Thornes)
Vygotsky, L.S.: *Thought and Language* (Cambridge)
Wragg, E.: *Classroom Management* (Routledge)
Wragg, E.: *Classroom Teaching Skills* (Routledge)

Index

activities 12–13; training 46; plenary 123–5, *see also* activities to objectives
activities to objectives 22–3
AFL (assessment for learning) 144–5, 147, *see also* assessment for learning
assertiveness 39
assessment: formative 144, summative 144
assessment for learning 58, 117–18, 144–9

BA (QTS) 15
B.Ed. 15
BSc (QTS) 15
behaviour management 24, 47
Bruner, J., *Towards a Theory of Instruction* 68–9

Capel, S. Leask, M. and Turner, T., *Learning to Teach in the Secondary School* 7, 65
career entry 150
choosing a course 14–18
choosing a school 153–7
classroom rules 31
collaborative work 55–6, 60
communication 31, 50
comparison 30, 32, 71
constructivism 67–70
creative 5
creativity 87

deadlines 35–6, 40, 74, 103–4, 111
defensiveness 39, 74
degree 14–15
depression 42, 46
DfES (Department for Education and Skills) 8, 10
Development Targets 151–2
differentiation 98–9, 128–31, 139–41, 143; by choice 136–7; by meta-language 132–3; by multiple access 133–6; by rotation 132–3; by teacher language 131, 140–1

entry profile 151
evaluation 21–2, 118–20; and action 126; and assessment 117–18; permanent 122–3
Every Child Matters 35
evidence 75–6
examples 72
extrinsic 23–5

feedback 56, *see also* lesson feedback
flexible PGCE see choosing a course
from teaching to learning 19–22

Gardner's multiple intelligences 66, 81, 13
graduate 15
group: discussion 109–13; roles 109–11

group emailing list 48
GTTR (Graduate Teacher Training
  Registry) 15, 18
GTP (Graduate Teacher Training
  Programme) 15, 18

inclusion 56, 66, 128–31, 143;
  more inclusion 137–9
induction 152
integration 16, 55
intended learning outcome see
  objectives
interactive 29, 121
internet 48
interview 160–6
intrinsic 23–5; methods 98

journey 29 see also key journeys

key journeys 19–27

learning objectives 10, 22–3, 25,
  56, 59, 87
learning styles 66
learning theory see theory
lesson: beginnings 31; feedback
  52–4; journey 68, 100–2;
  objectives 56; observations 77;
  planning 44–5, 56; plans 23,
  24; story 99
lessons 5, 23, 25
long-term plan 25

management skills 98
medium-term plan 25, 57, 58, 86
meetings 37; with teachers 13
mentor 30, 31, 39–40, 43–6,
  49–50, 50–5
meta-learning 141–3
motivation 2, 113
multiple access see differentiation
multiple intelligence 133–6,
  see also Gardner's multiple
  intelligences

National Curriculum 5, 6, 7, 9,
  10, 17
National Literacy Strategy 5
National Numeracy Strategy 5

NQT 152–3, 157

objectives 87–93; specific 46, 89,
  see also lesson objectives
observation 30–2, 43–4
observing lessons 12; teachers 12,
  25, 30–2
Ofsted website 155–6
organisation 26–7
outcome 104

pedagogy 35
peers 42; support 16, 47–8
PGCE (Postgraduate Teaching
  Qualification) see choosing a
  course
planning 22–5, 34, 46–7 57, 74–5,
  85–96, 165; backwards 86–7;
  0–24 planning 90, 92, 96; 0–60
  planning 88–90, 96
plans see lesson plans and
  planning
plenary 123–5
policies 36
powerbase 102
professional studies 3
professionalism 34–41
pupil shadowing 12

QCA (the Qualifications and
  Curriculum Authority) 9
QDO (Questions, Deadline,
  Outcome) 102–4
QTS (Qualified Teacher Status) 14,
  15, 75
questions 11–12, 44, 103–5
quietness 114

reading 7–8
reflection 16, 19, 21, 30–2, 39, 59
reflective: content 79–82 ; practice
  115; process 19, 32; style and
  structure 82–4; writing
  78–84
relationship 37–9
research 6, 7–8
rewards 62
rotation see differentiation
routines 30–1

scaffolding 68–9
scheme of work, 86, *see also*
    medium-term plans
school-based training *see* SCITT
SCITT (School-Centred Initial
    Teacher Training) *see* choosing
    a course
schools 35–6
school visit 11
Secondary Strategy 5, 10
select and self compare 7–10
short-term plan 25, 57, 58
show lesson 164–6
social constructivism 67–9
speaking and listening 102, 108
staffrooms 13
standards 75–8
Standards for Qualified Teacher
    Status 6, 10
Standards Site, the 10
strategies *see* National Literacy
    Strategy, National Numeracy
    Strategy and the Secondary
    Strategy
student teacher 34, 40
subject framework 10
subject knowledge 2–3, 7, 10, 35
    52

targets 43–6
task setting 102–4
teacher language 131, 140–1
Teachernet 10

teacher's day 32–3
teacher-self 30
teacher shadowing 12
teacher training 30, 42
teaching 5, 29, 51, 57, 59
teaching persona 29, 41
TDA (Training and Development
    Agency for Schools) 8, 17
TDA website 14, 150, 152
theory 16, 59, 64–70, 81
trainees 16–17, 19–23, 28, 33, 38,
    40, 58–9
transitions 56, 99–100

University-based training *see*
    choosing a course

valuing and validating pupil
    responses 105–6
Vygotsky, L. S., *Thought and
    Language* 67

websites: www.dfes.gov.uk 8; www.
    nc.uk.net 9; www.standards.
    dfes.gov.uk 10; www.tda.gov.
    uk 8; www.teachernet.gov.uk 10
    www.qca.org.uk 9; examination
    bodies 9
workload 4, 33–4, 46
work schemes 25

YAVA (You Ask, Volunteers Answer)
    107–8